6 Full-Length ACT Math Practice Tests

Extra Test Prep to Help Ace the ACT Math Test

By

Michael Smith & Reza Nazari

6 Full-Length ACT Math Practice Tests

Published in the United State of America By

The Math Notion

Web: WWW.MathNotion.Com

Email: info@Mathnotion.com

About the Author

Michael Smith has been a math instructor for over a decade now. He holds a master's degree in Management. Since 2006, Michael has devoted his time to both teaching and developing exceptional math learning materials. As a Math instructor and test prep expert, Michael has worked with thousands of students. He has used the feedback of his students to develop a unique study program that can be used by students to drastically improve their math score fast and effectively.

– SAT Math Practice Book

– ACT Math Practice Book

– GRE Math Practice Book

– Accuplacer Math Practice Book

– Common Core Math Practice Book

–many Math Education Workbooks, Exercise Books and Study Guides

As an experienced Math teacher, Mr. Smith employs a variety of formats to help students achieve their goals: He tutors online and in person, he teaches students in large groups, and he provides training materials and textbooks through his website and through Amazon.

You can contact Michael via email at:

info@Mathnotion.com

Prepare for the ACT Math test with a perfect practice book!

The surest way to practice your ACT Math test-taking skills is with simulated exams. This comprehensive practice book with 6 full length and realistic ACT Math practice tests help you measure your exam readiness, find your weak areas, and succeed on the ACT Math test. The detailed answers and explanations for each ACT Math question help you master every aspect of the ACT Math.

6 Full-length ACT Math Practice Tests is a prestigious resource to help you succeed on the ACT Math test. This perfect practice book features:

- Content 100% aligned with the ACT test
- Six full-length ACT Math practice tests like the actual test in length, format, question types, and degree of difficulty
- Detailed answers and explanations for the ACT Math practice questions
- Written by ACT Math top instructors and experts

After completing this hands-on exercise book, you will gain confidence, strong foundation, and adequate practice to succeed on the ACT Math test.

WWW.MathNotion.COM

… So Much More Online!

✓ FREE Math Lessons

✓ More Math Learning Books!

✓ Mathematics Worksheets

✓ Online Math Tutors

For a PDF Version of This Book

Please Visit WWW.MathNotion.com

Contents

ACT Math Test Review

Since 1959, the American College Testing Organization (ACT) has been judging student's potential regarding academics. ACT is a standardized test used for college admissions in the United States. In essence, it is a broad and quick assessment of students' academic abilities.

The ACT is divided into four major segments.

- English

- Reading

- Mathematics

- Science

The ACT also includes an optional 40-minute Writing Test.

In an ACT assessment test, all questions are weighted the same. You also have to keep in mind that the more difficult questions are randomly thrown around in the test. You can choose to skip over the more challenging tasks and ace out the simpler questions in the tests first.

There are 60 Mathematics questions on ACT and students have 60 minutes to answer the questions. The Mathematics section of the ACT contains multiple choice questions.

ACT Mathematics cover the following topics:

- Pre-Algebra (20-25%)

- Elementary Algebra (15-20%)

- Intermediate Algebra (15-20%)

- Coordinate Geometry (15-20%)

- Plane Geometry (20-25%)

- Trigonometry (5-10%)

ACT permits the use of personal calculators on the Math portion of the test.

In this section, there are two complete ACT Mathematics Tests. Take these tests to see what score you'll be able to receive on a real ACT test.

Time to Test

Time to refine your skill with a practice examination

Take a practice ACT Math Test to simulate the test day experience. After you've finished, score your test using the answer key.

Before You Start

- You'll need a pencil, a calculator and a timer to take the test.
- For each question, there are five possible answers. Choose which one is best.
- After you've finished the test, review the answer key to see where you went wrong.

Good Luck!

The hardest arithmetic to master is that which enables us to count our blessings.
~Eric Hoffer

ACT Math Practice Test Answer Sheets

Remove (or photocopy) these answer sheets and use them to complete the practice tests.

ACT Practice Test

1	Ⓐ Ⓑ Ⓒ Ⓓ Ⓔ	21	Ⓐ Ⓑ Ⓒ Ⓓ Ⓔ	41	Ⓐ Ⓑ Ⓒ Ⓓ Ⓔ
2	Ⓐ Ⓑ Ⓒ Ⓓ Ⓔ	22	Ⓐ Ⓑ Ⓒ Ⓓ Ⓔ	42	Ⓐ Ⓑ Ⓒ Ⓓ Ⓔ
3	Ⓐ Ⓑ Ⓒ Ⓓ Ⓔ	23	Ⓐ Ⓑ Ⓒ Ⓓ Ⓔ	43	Ⓐ Ⓑ Ⓒ Ⓓ Ⓔ
4	Ⓐ Ⓑ Ⓒ Ⓓ Ⓔ	24	Ⓐ Ⓑ Ⓒ Ⓓ Ⓔ	44	Ⓐ Ⓑ Ⓒ Ⓓ Ⓔ
5	Ⓐ Ⓑ Ⓒ Ⓓ Ⓔ	25	Ⓐ Ⓑ Ⓒ Ⓓ Ⓔ	45	Ⓐ Ⓑ Ⓒ Ⓓ Ⓔ
6	Ⓐ Ⓑ Ⓒ Ⓓ Ⓔ	26	Ⓐ Ⓑ Ⓒ Ⓓ Ⓔ	46	Ⓐ Ⓑ Ⓒ Ⓓ Ⓔ
7	Ⓐ Ⓑ Ⓒ Ⓓ Ⓔ	27	Ⓐ Ⓑ Ⓒ Ⓓ Ⓔ	47	Ⓐ Ⓑ Ⓒ Ⓓ Ⓔ
8	Ⓐ Ⓑ Ⓒ Ⓓ Ⓔ	28	Ⓐ Ⓑ Ⓒ Ⓓ Ⓔ	48	Ⓐ Ⓑ Ⓒ Ⓓ Ⓔ
9	Ⓐ Ⓑ Ⓒ Ⓓ Ⓔ	29	Ⓐ Ⓑ Ⓒ Ⓓ Ⓔ	49	Ⓐ Ⓑ Ⓒ Ⓓ Ⓔ
10	Ⓐ Ⓑ Ⓒ Ⓓ Ⓔ	30	Ⓐ Ⓑ Ⓒ Ⓓ Ⓔ	50	Ⓐ Ⓑ Ⓒ Ⓓ Ⓔ
11	Ⓐ Ⓑ Ⓒ Ⓓ Ⓔ	31	Ⓐ Ⓑ Ⓒ Ⓓ Ⓔ	51	Ⓐ Ⓑ Ⓒ Ⓓ Ⓔ
12	Ⓐ Ⓑ Ⓒ Ⓓ Ⓔ	32	Ⓐ Ⓑ Ⓒ Ⓓ Ⓔ	52	Ⓐ Ⓑ Ⓒ Ⓓ Ⓔ
13	Ⓐ Ⓑ Ⓒ Ⓓ Ⓔ	33	Ⓐ Ⓑ Ⓒ Ⓓ Ⓔ	53	Ⓐ Ⓑ Ⓒ Ⓓ Ⓔ
14	Ⓐ Ⓑ Ⓒ Ⓓ Ⓔ	34	Ⓐ Ⓑ Ⓒ Ⓓ Ⓔ	54	Ⓐ Ⓑ Ⓒ Ⓓ Ⓔ
15	Ⓐ Ⓑ Ⓒ Ⓓ Ⓔ	35	Ⓐ Ⓑ Ⓒ Ⓓ Ⓔ	55	Ⓐ Ⓑ Ⓒ Ⓓ Ⓔ
16	Ⓐ Ⓑ Ⓒ Ⓓ Ⓔ	36	Ⓐ Ⓑ Ⓒ Ⓓ Ⓔ	56	Ⓐ Ⓑ Ⓒ Ⓓ Ⓔ
17	Ⓐ Ⓑ Ⓒ Ⓓ Ⓔ	37	Ⓐ Ⓑ Ⓒ Ⓓ Ⓔ	57	Ⓐ Ⓑ Ⓒ Ⓓ Ⓔ
18	Ⓐ Ⓑ Ⓒ Ⓓ Ⓔ	38	Ⓐ Ⓑ Ⓒ Ⓓ Ⓔ	58	Ⓐ Ⓑ Ⓒ Ⓓ Ⓔ
19	Ⓐ Ⓑ Ⓒ Ⓓ Ⓔ	39	Ⓐ Ⓑ Ⓒ Ⓓ Ⓔ	59	Ⓐ Ⓑ Ⓒ Ⓓ Ⓔ
20	Ⓐ Ⓑ Ⓒ Ⓓ Ⓔ	40	Ⓐ Ⓑ Ⓒ Ⓓ Ⓔ	60	Ⓐ Ⓑ Ⓒ Ⓓ Ⓔ

ACT Practice Test 1

Mathematics

- ❖ 60 Questions.

- ❖ Total time for this test: 60 Minutes.

- ❖ You may use a scientific calculator on this test.

Administered *Month Year*

1) $7^{\frac{5}{3}} \times 7^{\frac{1}{3}} =?$

   A. 7^2 D. 7^1

   B. 7^1 E. 7^0

   C. 7^3

2) If $\frac{4x}{25} = \frac{x-1}{5}$, $x =?$

   A. $\frac{1}{4}$ D. 5

   B. $\frac{3}{4}$ E. $\frac{9}{4}$

   C. 3

3) 124 is equal to?

   A. $20 - (4 \times 10) + (6 \times 30)$

   B. $\left(\frac{11}{8} \times 72\right) + (\frac{125}{5})$

   C. $\left(\left(\frac{30}{4} + \frac{13}{2}\right) \times 7\right) - \frac{11}{2} + \frac{110}{4}$

   D. $(2 \times 10) + (50 \times 1.5) + 15$

   E. $\frac{481}{6} + \frac{121}{3}$

4) Six years ago, Amy was two times as old as Mike was. If Mike is 14 years old now, how old is Amy?

   A. 34   D. 20

   B. 28   E. 22

   C. 14

5) A number is chosen at random from 1 to 15. Find the probability of not selecting a composite number.

A. $\dfrac{1}{15}$

C. $\dfrac{7}{15}$

E. 0

B. 15

D. 5

6) If $|a| < 2$ then which of the following is true? $(b > 0)$?

  I. $-2b < ba < 2b$

  II. $-a < a^2 < a \quad if \ a < 0$

  III. $-7 < 2a - 3 < 1$

A. I only

C. I and III only

E. I, II and III

B. II only

D. III only

7) Removing which of the following numbers will change the average of the numbers to 8?

$$1, 4, 5, 8, 11, 12$$

A. 1

C. 5

E. 12

B. 4

D. 11

8) A rope weighs 700 grams per meter of length. What is the weight in kilograms of 13.2 meters of this rope? (1 kilograms = 1,000 grams)

A. 0.0924

C. 9.24

E. 92,400

B. 0.924

D. 9,240

9) If $y = 5ab + 2b^3$, what is y when $a = 3$ and $b = 1$?

   A. 22   C. 24   E. 17

   B. 26   D. 12

10) If $f(x) = 6 + x$ and $g(x) = -x^2 - 2 - 3x$, then find $(g - f)(x)$?

   A. $x^2 - 4x - 8$ C. $-x^2 - 4x + 8$ E. $-x^2 + 4x - 8$

   B. $x^2 - 4x + 8$ D. $-x^2 - 4x - 8$

11) The marked price of a computer is D dollar. Its price decreased by 40% in January and later increased by 10 % in February. What is the final price of the computer in D dollar?

   A. 0.60 D   C. 0.70 D   E. 1.80 D

   B. 0.66 D   D. 1.60 D

12) The number 60.5 is 1,000 times greater than which of the following numbers?

   A. 0.605   C. 0.0650   E. 0.000605

   B. 0.0605   D. 0.00605

13) David's current age is 44 years, and Ava's current age is 8 years. In how many years David's age will be 4 times Ava's age?

   A. 4   C. 8   E. 14

   B. 6   D. 10

14) How many tiles of 8 cm² is needed to cover a floor of dimension 7 cm by 32 cm?

    A. 15   C. 20   E. 32

    B. 18   D. 28

15) What is the median of these numbers? 3, 8, 17, 7, 15, 21, 6

    A. 8   C. 17   E. 21

    B. 6   D. 15

16) A company pays its employer \$8000 plus 3% of all sales profit. If x is the number of all sales profit, which of the following represents the employer's revenue?

    A. $0.03x$ C. $0.03x + 8000$ E. $-0.97x - 8000$

    B. $0.97x - 8000$ D. $0.97x + 8000$

17) What is the area of a square whose diagonal is 6 cm?

    A. 16 cm²   C. 36 cm²   E. 216 cm²

    B. 18 cm²   D. 33 cm²

18) What is the value of x in the following figure?

    A. 150

    B. 165

    C. 135

    D. 95

    E. 105

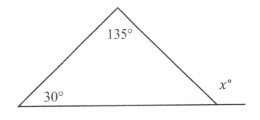

19) Right triangle ABC is shown below. Which of the following is true for all possible values of angle A and B?

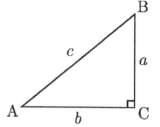

A. $\tan A = \tan B$

B. $\tan^2 A = \tan^2 B$

C. $\tan A = 1$

D. $\sin A = \cos B$

E. $\cot A = \sin B$

20) What is the value of y in the following system of equation?

$$4x - 2y = -20$$

$$-x + y = 10$$

A. – 4

B. – 2

C. 4

D. 5

E. 10

21) How long does a 430–miles trip take moving at 50 miles per hour (mph)?

A. 4 hours

B. 6 hours and 36 minutes

C. 8 hours and 36 minutes

D. 8 hours and 30 minutes

E. 10 hours and 30 minutes

22) From the figure, which of the following must be true? (figure not drawn to scale)

A. $y = z$

B. $y = 4x$

C. $y \geq x$

D. $y + 3x = z$

E. $y > x$

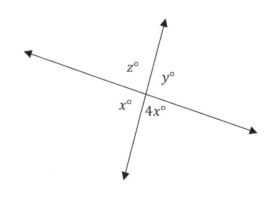

23) Which is the correct statement?

   A. $\frac{1}{4} > 0.15$

   B. $10\% = \frac{3}{5}$

   C. $3 < \frac{3}{2}$

   D. $\frac{4}{6} > 0.6$

   E. None of them above

24) When 30% of 80 is added to 18% of 800, the resulting number is:

   A. 36

   B. 95

   C. 168

   D. 120

   E. 175

25) A ladder leans against a wall forming a 60° angle between the ground and the ladder. If the bottom of the ladder is 40 feet away from the wall, how long is the ladder?

   A. 40 feet

   B. 60 feet

   C. 50 feet

   D. 80 feet

   E. 160 feet

26) If 60 % of a class are girls, and 15 % of girls play tennis, what percent of the class play tennis?

   A. 9 %

   B. 12%

   C. 15 %

   D. 30 %

   E. 60 %

27) If x is a real number, and if $x^3 + 18 = 140$, then x lies between which two consecutive integers?

   A. 1 and 2

   B. 2 and 3

   C. 3 and 4

   D. 4 and 5

   E. 5 and 6

28) If $(x - 2)^3 = 8$ which of the following could be the value of $(x - 3)(x - 2)$?

    A. 1   C. 6   E. −2

    B. 2   D. −1

29) Simplify.

$$3x^2 + 4y^5 - x^2 + 3z^3 - 2y^2 + 3x^3 - 3y^5 + 4z^3$$

A. $3x^2 - 2y^2 + y^5 + 7z^3$

B. $2x^2 + 3x^3 - 2y^2 + y^5 + 7z^3$

C. $2x^2 + 3x^3 + 3y^5 + 7z^3$

D. $2x^2 + 3x^3 - 2y^2 + 5y^5 + 7z^3$

E. $2x^2 + 3x^3 - 2y^2 + 7z^3$

30) In five successive hours, a car travels 40 km, 42 km, 55 km, 38 km and 50 km. In the next five hours, it travels with an average speed of 60 km per hour. Find the total distance the car traveled in 10 hours.

    A. 525 km   C. 468 km   E. 1,000 km

    B. 430 km   D. 510 km

31) From last year, the price of gasoline has increased from $1.15 per gallon to $1.38 per gallon. The new price is what percent of the original price?

    A. 72 %   C. 140 %   E. 180 %

    B. 120 %   D. 160 %

32) Simplify $(-4 + 8i)(3 + 5i)$,

    A. $6 - 2i$ D. $-52 + 2i$

    B. $52 - 2i$ E. $2i$

    C. $6 + 2i$

33) If $\tan \theta = \frac{3}{4}$ and $\sin \theta > 0$, then $\cos \theta = ?$

    A. $-\frac{4}{5}$ D. $-\frac{12}{5}$

    B. $\frac{4}{5}$ E. 0

    C. $\frac{5}{12}$

34) Which of the following has the same period and two times the amplitude of

graph $y = \cos x$?

    A. $y = \cos 2x$ D. $y = 2 + 2\cos x$

    B. $y = \cos (x + 2)$ E. $y = 4 + \cos x$

    C. $y = 4\cos 2x$

35) Which of the following shows the numbers in increasing order?

    A. $\frac{1}{3}, \frac{7}{11}, \frac{4}{7}, \frac{3}{4}$ D. $\frac{7}{11}, \frac{3}{4}, \frac{4}{7}, \frac{1}{3}$

    B. $\frac{1}{3}, \frac{4}{7}, \frac{7}{11}, \frac{3}{4}$ E. None of them above

    C. $\frac{4}{7}, \frac{3}{4}, \frac{7}{11}, \frac{1}{3}$

36) In 1999, the average worker's income increased $2,000 per year starting from $22,000 annual salary. Which equation represents income greater than average? (I = income, x = number of years after 1999)

A. $I > 2{,}000\,x + 22{,}000$

B. $I > -\,2{,}000\,x + 22{,}000$

C. $I < -2{,}000\,x + 22{,}000$

D. $I < 2{,}000\,x - 22{,}000$

E. $I < 24{,}000\,x + 22{,}000$

Questions 37 to 39 are based on the following data

The result of a research shows the number of men and women in four cities of a country.

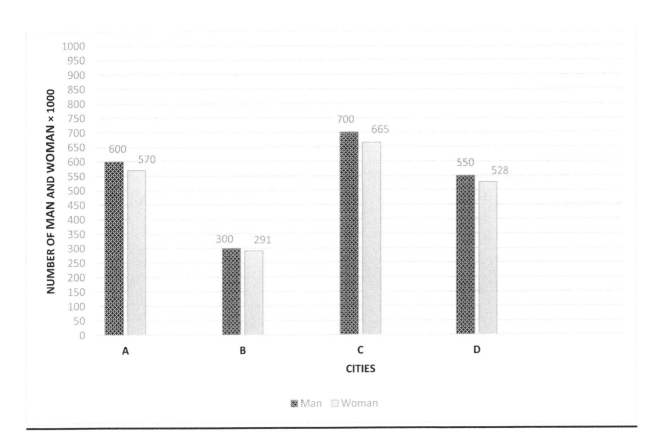

37) What's the ratio of percentage of men in city C to percentage of men in city B?

    A. 0.10   C. 0.99   E. 1.00

    B. 0.01   D. 1.01

38) What's the minimum ratio of woman to man in the four cities?

    A. 0.97   C. 0.95   E. 0.96

    B. 0.98   D. 0.99

39) How many women should be added to city D until the ratio of women to men will be 1.3?

    A. 122   C. 148   E. 135

    B. 187   D. 192

40) What are the values of mode and median in the following set of numbers?

$$1, 2, 4, 5, 4, 4, 3, 3, 3, 2, 1$$

    A. Mode: 1, 2 Median: 4   D. Mode: 1, 3 Median: 4

    B. Mode: 3, 4 Median: 3   E. Mode: 3, Median: 3

    C. Mode: 2, 4 Median: 3

41) x is $y\%$ of what number?

    A. $\dfrac{x}{100y}$ C. $\dfrac{100x}{y}$ E. $\dfrac{xy}{100}$

    B. $\dfrac{y}{100x}$ D. $\dfrac{100y}{x}$

42) If cotangent of an angel β is 1, then the tangent of angle β is

    A. -1 C. 0   E. $-\dfrac{1}{2}$

    B. 1   D. $\dfrac{1}{2}$

43) If a box contains red and blue balls in ratio of 3: 4, how many red balls are there if 80 blue balls are in the box?

    A. 90   C. 30   E. 8

    B. 60   D. 10

44) 4 liters of water are poured into an aquarium that's 20cm long, 5cm wide, and 50cm high. How many cm will the water level in the aquarium rise due to this added water? (1 liter of water = 1,000 cm^3)

A. 80   C. 50   E. 4

B. 40   D. 10

45) What is the surface area of the cylinder below?

A. $36 \pi \text{ in}^2$

B. $36 \pi^2 \text{in}^2$

C. $88 \pi \text{ in}^2$

D. $88 \pi^2 \text{in}^2$

E. $56 \pi \text{ in}^2$

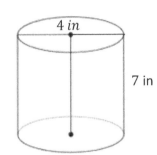

4 in

7 in

46) A chemical solution contains 3% alcohol. If there is 21ml of alcohol, what is the volume of the solution?

A. 320 ml   C. 700 ml   E. 1,400 ml

B. 350 ml   D. 1,200 ml

47) What is the solution of the following inequality?

$$|x - 8| \leq 2$$

A. $x \geq 10 \cup x \leq 6$ D. $x \leq 6$

B. $6 \leq x \leq 10$ E. Set of real numbers

C. $x \geq 10$

48) Which of the following points lies on the line $4x - y = -3$?

    A. $(3, -1)$ C. $(-1, -1)$ E. $(0, -3)$

    B. $(-1, 3)$ D. $(3, -3)$

49) In the following figure, ABCD is a rectangle, and E and F are points on AD and DC, respectively. The area of ΔBED is 10, and the area of ΔBDF is 12. What is the perimeter of the rectangle?

    A. 20

    B. 22

    C. 32

    D. 40

    E. 44

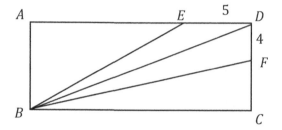

50) In the xy-plane, the point $(5,6)$ and $(4,5)$ are on the line A. Which of the following equations of lines is parallel to line A?

    A. $y = 3x$ C. $y = \frac{x}{2}$ E. $y = x$

    B. $y = 10$ D. $y = 2x$

51) When point A $(6, 2)$ is reflected over the y-axis to get the point B, what are the coordinates of point B?

    A. $(6, 2)$ C. $(-6, 2)$ E. $(0, 2)$

    B. $(-6, -2)$ D. $(6, -2)$

52) A bag contains 16 balls: two green, five black, eight blue, a brown, a red and one white. If 15 balls are removed from the bag at random, what is the probability that a brown ball has been removed?

A. $\frac{1}{3}$

B. $\frac{1}{6}$

C. $\frac{16}{15}$

D. $\frac{15}{16}$

E. $\frac{1}{2}$

53) If a tree casts a 48–foot shadow at the same time that a 5 feet yardstick casts a 3–foot shadow, what is the height of the tree?

A. 14 ft

B. 30 ft

C. 80ft

D. 48 ft

E. 52 ft

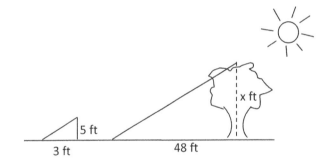

54) If the area of trapezoid is 96, what is the perimeter of the trapezoid?

A. 37

B. 42

C. 53

D. 57

E. 63

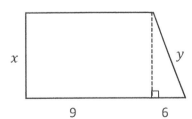

55) If 60% of x equal to 20% of 30, then what is the value of $(x + 2)^2$?

    A. 12.20   C. 25.01   E. 144

    B. 24   D. 1810

56) If $f(x) = 2x^3 + 5x^2 + 2x$ and $g(x) = -1$, what is the value of $f(g(x))$?

    A. 18   C. 14   E. 0

    B. 23   D. 1

57) A boat sails 120 miles south and then 50 miles east. How far is the boat from its start point?

    A. 35 miles   C. 80 miles   E. 50 miles

    B. 130 miles   D. 100 miles

58) If $x \begin{bmatrix} 2 & 0 \\ 0 & 6 \end{bmatrix} = \begin{bmatrix} x + 3y - 5 & 0 \\ 0 & 8y + 10 \end{bmatrix}$, what is the product of x and y?

    A. 1   C. 7   E. 28

    B. 4   D. 22

59) If $f(x) = 2^x$ and $g(x) = log_2 x$, which of the following expressions is equal to $f(2g(p))$?

    A. $2P$ C. p^2 E. $\frac{p}{2}$

    B. 2^p D. p^4

60) In the following equation when z is divided by 5, what is the effect on x?

$$x = \frac{8y + \frac{r}{r+1}}{\frac{10}{z}}$$

A. x is divided by 3

B. x is divided by 5

C. x does not change

D. x is multiplied by 5

E. x is multiplied by 3

STOP

This is the End of this Test. You may check your work on this Test if you still have time.

ACT Practice Test 2

Mathematics

- ❖ **60 Questions.**

- ❖ **Total time for this test: 60 Minutes.**

- ❖ **You may use a scientific calculator on this test.**

Administered *Month Year*

1) Convert 840,000 to scientific notation.

   A. 8.40×1000 D. 8.4×10^5

   B. 8.40×10^{-5} E. 8.4×10^4

   C. 8.4×100

2) $(x^6)^{\frac{5}{8}}$ equal to?

   A. $x^{\frac{15}{4}}$ C. $x^{\frac{4}{15}}$ E. $x^{\frac{5}{48}}$

   B. $x^{\frac{53}{8}}$ D. $x^{\frac{8}{53}}$

3) Simplify $\frac{2-5i}{-2i}$?

   A. $\frac{5}{2} + i$ C. $\frac{1}{2} - i$ E. i

   B. $\frac{3}{2} - i$ D. $\frac{1}{2} + i$

4) What is the value of x in the following equation?

$$5^x = 625$$

   A. 3   C. 5   E. 7

   B. 4   D. 6

5) What is the sum of prime numbers between 10 and 20?

   A. 73   C. 70   E. 120

   B. 52   D. 60

6) If $\sqrt{7x} = \sqrt{y}$, then $x =$?

A. $7y$

C. y^2

E. $\frac{y}{7}$

B. $\sqrt{\frac{y}{7}}$

D. $\sqrt{7y}$

7) The average weight of 20 girls in a class is 60 kg and the average weight of 30 boys in the same class is 65 kg. What is the average weight of all the 50 students in that class?

A. 60

C. 61.28

E. 62.48

B. 63

D. 62.90

8) If $y = (-2x^3)^2$, which of the following expressions is equal to y?

A. $-3x^5$

C. $3x^5$

E. $4x^6$

B. $-3x^6$

D. $4x^5$

9) What is the value of the expression $3(x - y) + (1 - x)^2$ when $x = 3$ and $= -4$?

A. $- 8$

C. 25

E. 76

B. 18

D. 48

10) Sophia purchased a sofa for $399.75. The sofa is regularly priced at $615. What was the percent discount Sophia received on the sofa?

A. 1.35%

C. 54%

E. 1.54%

B. 35%

D. 65%

11) If $f(x) = 2x - 1$ and $g(x) = x^2 - 2x$, then find $(\frac{f}{g})(x)$.

A. $\dfrac{2x-1}{x^2-2x}$

C. $\dfrac{x-1}{x^2-1}$

E. $\dfrac{x^2-2x}{2x-1}$

B. $\dfrac{x-1}{x^2-2x}$

D. $\dfrac{2x+1}{x^2+2x}$

12) In the standard (x, y) coordinate plane, which of the following lines contains

the points $(3, -5)$ and $(8, 10)$?

A. $y = 3x - 14$

D. $y = -\dfrac{1}{3}x + 14$

B. $y = \dfrac{1}{3}x + 14$

E. $y = 3x - 11$

C. $y = -3x + 7$

13) A bank is offering 2.5% simple interest on a savings account. If you deposit

$15,000, how much interest will you earn in two years?

A. $450

C. $4,500

E. $4,600

B. $750

D. $6,400

14) If the ratio of home fans to visiting fans in a crowd is 2:3 and all 25,000 seats

in a stadium are filled, how many visiting fans are in attendance?

A. 100,000

C. 1,000

E. 15,000

B. 100

D. 10

15) If the interior angles of a quadrilateral are in the ratio 1:2:4:5, what is the measure of the largest angle?

   A. 30°   C. 108°   E. 150°

   B. 60°   D. 120°

16) If $x + sin^2a + cos^2a = 3$, then $x =$?

   A. 1   C. 3   E. 5

   B. 2   D. 4

17) If the area of a circle is 81 square meters, what is its diameter?

   A. 9π C. $\frac{9\sqrt{\pi}}{\pi}$ E. $9\sqrt{\pi}$

   B. $\frac{9}{\pi}$ D. $81\pi^2$

18) The length of a rectangle is $\frac{3}{4}$ times its width. If the width is 24, what is the perimeter of this rectangle?

   A. 38   C. 84   E. 150

   B. 48   D. 169

19) In the figure below, line A is parallel to line B. What is the value of angle x?

   A. 35 degree

   B. 55 degree

   C. 85 degree

   D. 105 degree

   E. 125 degree

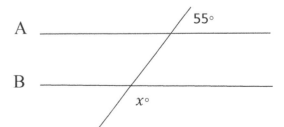

20) What is the value of x in the following system of equations?

$$2x + 3y = 10$$
$$6x - 3y = -18$$

A. -1 C. -2 E. 8

B. 1   D. 4

21) An angle is equal to one eighth of its supplement. What is the measure of that angle?

A. 20   C. 30   E. 45

B. 22.5   D. 44.5

22) Last week 28,000 fans attended a football match. This week three times as many bought tickets, but one sixth of them cancelled their tickets. How many are attending this week?

A. 9,000   C. 56,000   E. 84,000

B. 42,000   D. 70,000

23) If $sin\alpha = \frac{1}{2}$ in a right triangle and the angle α is an acute angle, then what is $cos\ \alpha$?

A. $\frac{\sqrt{6}}{2}$ C. $\sqrt{3}$ E. $\frac{\sqrt{3}}{2}$

B. $\frac{2}{3}$ D. $\frac{4}{\sqrt{3}}$

24) In following rectangle which statement is true?

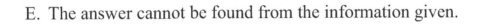

    A. AB is parallel to BC

    B. AB is perpendicular to DC

    C. Length of AB equal to half of length BC

    D. The measure of all the angles equals 360°.

    E. The answer cannot be found from the information given.

25) In the standard (x, y) coordinate system plane, what is the area of the circle

with the following equation?

$$(x + 2)^2 + (y - 4)^2 = 9$$

    A. 3π C. 8π E. 2π

    B. 9π D. 4π

26) In two successive years, the population of a town is increased by 15% and 20%.

What percent of the population is increased after two years?

    A. 32%   C. 38%   E. 70%

    B. 35%   D. 68%

27) Simplify.

$$4x^2y^3 + 5x^3y^5 - (5x^2y^3 - 2x^3y^5)$$

    A. $-x^2y^3$ C. $7x^2y^3$ E. $6x^5y^8$

    B. $6x^2y^3 - x^3y^5$ D. $7x^3y^5 - x^2y^3$

28) What are the zeroes of the function $f(x) = x^3 + 5x^2 + 6x$?

A. 0

C. 0, 2, 3

E. 0, -2, -3

B. -2, -3

D. -1, -3

29) If one angle of a right triangle measures $60°$, what is the sine of the other acute angle?

A. $\frac{1}{2}$

C. $\frac{\sqrt{3}}{2}$

E. $\sqrt{3}$

B. $\frac{\sqrt{2}}{2}$

D. 1

30) In the following figure, what is the perimeter of $\triangle ABC$ if the area of $\triangle ADC$ is 15?

A. 37.5

B. 21

C. 15

D. 24

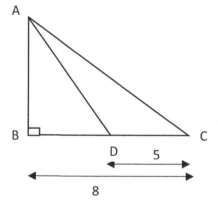

E. The answer cannot be determined from the information given

31) Which of the following is one solution of this equation?

$$x^2 + 2x - 5 = 0$$

A. $\sqrt{2} + 1$

C. $\sqrt{6} - 1$

E. $\sqrt{12}$

B. $\sqrt{2} - 1$

D. $\sqrt{6} + 1$

32) Two-kilograms apple and three-kilograms orange cost $34.2. If one-kilogram

apple costs $3.6 how much does one-kilogram orange cost?

A. $9   C. $5.5   E. $4

B. $6   D. $5

33) Which of the following expressions is equal to $\sqrt{\dfrac{x^2}{3} + \dfrac{x^2}{9}}$?

A. x C. $x\sqrt{x}$ E. $2x$

B. $\dfrac{2x}{3}$ D. $\dfrac{x\sqrt{x}}{2}$

Questions 34 to 36 are based on the following data

Number of clothes sold in a clothing store

34) Between which two of the months shown was there a twenty percent increase in the number of pants sold?

A. January and February

B. February and March

C. March and April

D. April and May

E. May and June

35) During the six-month period shown, what is the mean number of shirts and median number of shoes per month?

A. 25, 147.5

B. 149, 25

C. 149, 30

D. 30, 147.5

E. 30, 25

36) How many shoes need to be added in April until the ratio of number of pants to number of shoes in April equals to five-twelfth of this ratio in May?

    A. 20   C. 25   E. 40

    B. 30   D. 35

37) A card is drawn at random from a standard 52–card deck, what is the probability that the card is of diamonds? (The deck includes 13 of each suit clubs, diamonds, hearts, and spades)

    A. $\dfrac{1}{3}$ C. $\dfrac{1}{6}$ E. $\dfrac{1}{104}$

    B. $\dfrac{1}{4}$ D. $\dfrac{1}{52}$

38) A football team had \$30,000 to spend on supplies. The team spent \$24,000 on new balls. New sport shoes cost \$140 each. Which of the following inequalities represent how many new shoes the team can purchase?

    A. $140x + 24{,}000 \le 30{,}000$ D. $24{,}000x + 140 \ge 30{,}000$

    B. $140x + 24{,}000 \ge 30{,}000$ E. $24{,}000x + 1400 \ge 30{,}000$

    C. $24{,}000x + 140 \le 30{,}000$

39) If $x = 9$, what is the value of y in the following equation?

$$3y = \frac{2x^2}{3} + 6$$

    A. 20   C. 60   E. 150

    B. 35   D. 110

40) A swimming pool holds 3,000 cubic feet of water. The swimming pool is 15 feet long and 10 feet wide. How deep is the swimming pool?

A. 6 feet   C. 8 feet   E. 20 feet

B. 4 feet   D. 10 feet

41) The ratio of boys to girls in a school is 2:6. If there are 800 students in a school, how many boys are in the school.

A. 540   C. 800   E. 200

B. 500   D. 600

42) If $(x - 3)^2 + 1 > 3x - 1$, then x can equal which of the following?

A. 2   C. 8   E. 4

B. 6   D. 3

43) Let r and p be constants. If $x^2 + 4x + r$ factors into $(x + 3)(x + p)$, the values of r and p respectively are?

A. 3, 1   C. 2, 3

B. 1, 3   D. 3, 2

E. The answer cannot be found from the information given.

44) If 120 % of a number is 72, then what is 80 % of that number?

A. 45   C. 48   E. 80

B. 50   D. 55

45) The width of a box is one third of its length. The height of the box is one third of its width. If the length of the box is 36 cm, what is the volume of the box?

A. 144 cm³

B. 324 cm³

C. 576 cm³

D. 1,728 cm³

E. 2,704 cm³

46) The average of five consecutive numbers is 36. What is the smallest number?

A. 38

B. 36

C. 34

D. 12

E. 8

47) The surface area of a cylinder is $120\pi\ cm^2$. If its height is 7 cm, what is the radius of the cylinder?

A. 13 cm

B. 11 cm

C. 12 cm

D. 5 cm

E. 7 cm

48) In a coordinate plane, triangle ABC has coordinates: $(4, -2)$, $(-2, -3)$, and $(3,5)$. If triangle ABC is reflected over the y-axis, what are the coordinates of the new image?

A. $(4, -2), (-2, -3), (3,5)$

B. $(-2, 4), (-3, -2), (5, 3)$

C. $(-4, -2), (2, -3), (-3,5)$

D. $(4, -2), (-2,3), (3, -5)$

E. $(-2, -4), (3,2), (-5, -3)$

49) What is the slope of a line that is perpendicular to the line $8x - 4y = 16$?

    A. -2 C. 4 E. 14

    B. $-\dfrac{1}{2}$ D. 12

50) What is the difference in area between a 8 cm by 5 cm rectangle and a circle with diameter of 12 cm? ($\pi = 3$)

    A. 56 C. 8 E. 3

    B. 68 D. 6

51) If $f(x) = 3x^3 + 3$ and $(x) = \dfrac{1}{x}$, what is the value of $f(g(x))$?

    A. $\dfrac{1}{3x^3 + 3}$ C. $\dfrac{1}{3x}$ E. $\dfrac{3}{x^3} + 3$

    B. $\dfrac{3}{x^3}$ D. $\dfrac{1}{3x + 3}$

52) A cruise line ship left Port A and traveled 50 miles due west and then 120 miles due north. At this point, what is the shortest distance from the cruise to port A?

    A. 70 miles   C. 150 miles   E. 230 miles

    B. 80 miles   D. 130 miles

53) The length of a rectangle is 2 meters greater than 3 times its width. The perimeter of the rectangle is 36 meters. What is the area of the rectangle?

    A. 16 m^2 C. 56 m^2 E. 110 m^2

    B. 36 m^2 D. 72 m^2

54) Tickets to a movie cost $12.50 for adults and $6.50 for students. A group of 16 friends purchased tickets for $128. How many student tickets did they buy?

A. 4   C. 6   E. 8

B. 12   D. 10

55) What is the solution of the following inequality?

$$|x - 2| \geq 4$$

A. $x \geq 6 \cup x \leq -2$ D. $x \leq -2$

B. $-2 \leq x \leq 6$ E. Set of real numbers

C. $x \geq 6$

56) If $\tan x = \frac{5}{12}$, then $\sin x =$?

A. $\frac{1}{2}$ C. $\frac{12}{13}$

B. $\frac{5}{13}$ D. $\frac{7}{12}$

E. It cannot be determined from the information given.

57) In the following figure, ABCD is a rectangle. If $a = \sqrt{3}$, and $b = 4a$, find the area of the shaded region. (the shaded region is a trapezoid)

A. 12

B. 20

C. $10\sqrt{3}$

D. $20\sqrt{3}$

E. $12\sqrt{3}$

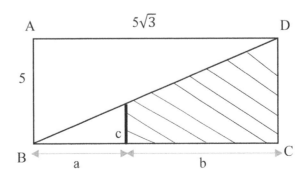

58) If the ratio of $7a$ to $3b$ is $\frac{1}{15}$, what is the ratio of a to b?

A. 15

B. 35

C. $\frac{1}{35}$

D. $\frac{1}{30}$

E. $\frac{1}{15}$

59) If $A = \begin{bmatrix} -1 & 3 \\ 1 & -3 \end{bmatrix}$ and $B = \begin{bmatrix} 5 & 1 \\ -3 & 4 \end{bmatrix}$, then $2A - B =$

A. $\begin{bmatrix} -4 & 1 \\ 3 & -5 \end{bmatrix}$

B. $\begin{bmatrix} -2 & 4 \\ 2 & -4 \end{bmatrix}$

C. $\begin{bmatrix} 2 & 3 \\ -1 & 1 \end{bmatrix}$

D. $\begin{bmatrix} 1 & 5 \\ 0 & -1 \end{bmatrix}$

E. $\begin{bmatrix} -7 & 5 \\ 5 & -10 \end{bmatrix}$

60) What is the amplitude of the graph of the equation $y - 1 = 3cos2x$? (half the distance between the graph's minimum and maximum y-values in standard (x, y) coordinate plane is the amplitude of a graph.)

A. 6

B. 3

C. 2

D. 1

E. 0.5

STOP

This is the End of this Test. You may check your work on this Test if you still have time.

ACT Practice Test 3

Mathematics

- ❖ **60 Questions.**

- ❖ **Total time for this test: 60 Minutes**.

- ❖ **You may use a scientific calculator on this test.**

Administered *Month Year*

1) $4^{\frac{7}{3}} \times 4^{\frac{2}{3}} = ?$

   A. 4^2 D. 4^4

   B. 4 E. 4^0

   C. 4^3

2) If $\frac{4x}{25} = \frac{x-1}{5}$, $x = ?$

   A. $\frac{1}{4}$ C. 3

                                D. 5

   B. $\frac{3}{4}$

                                E. $\frac{9}{4}$

3) 124 is equal to?

   A. $20 - (4 \times 10) + (6 \times 30)$

   B. $\left(\frac{11}{8} \times 72\right) + \left(\frac{125}{5}\right)$

   C. $\left(\left(\frac{30}{4} + \frac{13}{2}\right) \times 7\right) - \frac{11}{2} + \frac{110}{4}$

   D. $(2 \times 10) + (50 \times 1.5) + 15$

   E. $\frac{481}{6} + \frac{121}{3}$

4) Six years ago, Amy was two times as old as Mike was. If Mike is 14 years old now, how old is Amy?

   A. 34   D. 20

   B. 28   E. 22

   C. 14

5) A number is chosen at random from 1 to 10. Find the probability of not selecting a composite number.

A. $\frac{1}{10}$

C. $\frac{2}{5}$

E. 0

B. 10

D. 1

6) If $|a| < 2$ then which of the following is true? $(b > 0)$?

IV. $-2b < ba < 2b$

V. $-a < a^2 < a \quad if \ a < 0$

VI. $-7 < 2a - 3 < 1$

A. I only

C. I and III only

E. I, II and III

B. II only

D. III only

7) Removing which of the following numbers will change the average of the numbers to 6?

$$1, 4, 5, 8, 11, 12$$

A. 11

C. 5

E. 12

B. 4

D. 11

8) A rope weighs 600 grams per meter of length. What is the weight in kilograms of 14.2 meters of this rope? (1 kilograms = 1,000 grams)

A. 0.0852

C. 8.52

E. 85,200

B. 0.852

D. 8,520

9) If $y = 4ab + 3b^3$, what is y when $a = 3$ and $b = 1$?

   A. 22   C. 24   E. 15

   B. 26   D. 12

10) If $f(x) = 8 + x$ and $g(x) = -x^2 - 5 - 4x$, then find $(g - f)(x)$?

   A. $x^2 - 5x - 13$ C. $-x^2 - 5x + 13$ E. $-x^2 + 5x - 13$

   B. $x^2 - 5x + 13$ D. $-x^2 - 5x - 13$

11) The marked price of a computer is D dollar. Its price decreased by 60% in January and later increased by 10 % in February. What is the final price of the computer in D dollar?

   A. 0.40 D   C. 0.70 D   E. 1.80 D

   B. 0.44 D   D. 1.40 D

12) The number 80.5 is 1,000 times greater than which of the following numbers?

   A. 0.805   C. 0.0850   E. 0.000805

   B. 0.0805   D. 0.00805

13) David's current age is 44 years, and Ava's current age is 8 years. In how many years David's age will be 4 times Ava's age?

   A. 4   C. 8   E. 14

   B. 6   D. 10

14) How many tiles of 9 cm² is needed to cover a floor of dimension 8 cm by 36 cm?

    A. 15   C. 20   E. 36

    B. 18   D. 32

15) What is the median of these numbers? 4, 9, 18, 8, 16, 22, 7

    A. 9   C. 18   E. 22

    B. 7   D. 16

16) A company pays its employer $7,000 plus 5% of all sales profit. If x is the number of all sales profit, which of the following represents the employer's revenue?

    A. $0.05x$ C. $0.05x + 7,000$ E. $-0.95x - 7,000$

    B. $0.95x - 7,000$ D. $0.95x + 7,000$

17) What is the area of a square whose diagonal is 8 cm?

    A. 64 cm²   C. 36 cm²   E. 216 cm²

    B. 32 cm²   D. 18 cm²

18) What is the value of x in the following figure?

    A. 150

    B. 175

    C. 135

    D. 95

    E. 105

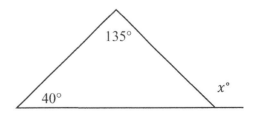

19) Right triangle ABC is shown below. Which of the following is true for all possible values of angle A and B?

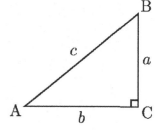

A. $tan\ A = tan\ B$

B. $tan^2 A = tan^2 B$

C. $tan\ A = 1$

D. $sin\ A = cos\ B$

E. $cot\ A = sin B$

20) What is the value of y in the following system of equation?

$$4x - 3y = -12$$

$$-x + y = 4$$

A. – 4

B. – 2

C. 8

D. 5

E. 4

21) How long does a 248–miles trip take moving at 40 miles per hour (mph)?

A. 4 hours

B. 6 hours and 36 minutes

C. 6 hours and 18 minutes

D. 8 hours and 30 minutes

E. 10 hours and 30 minutes

22) From the figure, which of the following must be true? (figure not drawn to scale)

A. $y = z$

B. $y = 6x$

C. $y \geq x$

D. $y + 5x = z$

E. $y > x$

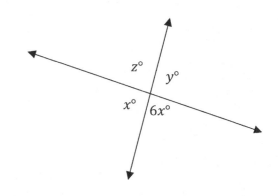

23) Which is the correct statement?

A. $\frac{1}{4} < 0.15$

D. $\frac{4}{6} > 0.6$

B. $10\% = \frac{3}{5}$

E. None of them above

C. $3 < \frac{3}{2}$

24) When 40% of 60 is added to 16% of 600, the resulting number is:

A. 36

C. 120

E. 175

B. 95

D. 156

25) A ladder leans against a wall forming a 60° angle between the ground and the ladder. If the bottom of the ladder is 40 feet away from the wall, how long is the ladder?

A. 40 feet

C. 50 feet

E. 160 feet

B. 60 feet

D. 80 feet

26) If 80% of a class are girls, and 15% of girls play tennis, what percent of the class play tennis?

A. 12%

C. 15%

E. 60%

B. 9%

D. 30%

27) If x is a real number, and if $x^3 + 28 = 120$, then x lies between which two consecutive integers?

A. 1 and 2

C. 3 and 4

E. 5 and 6

B. 2 and 3

D. 4 and 5

28) If $(x-3)^3 = 8$ which of the following could be the value of $(x-3)(x-2)$?

A. 1   C. 6   E. −2

B. 2   D. −1

29) Simplify.

$$3x^2 + 4y^5 - x^2 + 3z^3 - 2y^2 + 3x^3 - 3y^5 + 4z^3$$

A. $3x^2 - 2y^2 + y^5 + 7z^3$

B. $2x^2 + 3x^3 - 2y^2 + y^5 + 7z^3$

C. $2x^2 + 3x^3 + 3y^5 + 7z^3$

D. $2x^2 + 3x^3 - 2y^2 + 5y^5 + 7z^3$

E. $2x^2 + 3x^3 - 2y^2 + 7z^3$

30) In five successive hours, a car travels 40 km, 42 km, 55 km, 38 km and 50 km. In the next five hours, it travels with an average speed of 60 km per hour. Find the total distance the car traveled in 10 hours.

A. 525 km   C. 468 km   E. 1,000 km

B. 430 km   D. 510 km

31) From last year, the price of gasoline has increased from $1.15 per gallon to $1.61 per gallon. The new price is what percent of the original price?

A. 72%   C. 120%   E. 180%

B. 140%   D. 160%

32) Simplify $(-3 + 4i)(4 + 5i)$,

A. $6 - i$

B. $32 - i$

C. $6 + i$

D. $-32 + i$

E. i

33) If $tan\ \theta = \frac{6}{8}$ and $sin\ \theta > 0$, then $cos\ \theta = ?$

A. $-\frac{4}{5}$

B. $\frac{4}{5}$

C. $\frac{5}{12}$

D. $-\frac{12}{5}$

E. 0

34) Which of the following has the same period and two times the amplitude of graph $y = cosx$?

A. $y = cos\ 2x$

B. $y = cos\ (x + 2)$

C. $y = 4\cos 2x$

D. $y = 2 + 2\ cos\ x$

E. $y = 4 + cos\ x$

35) Which of the following shows the numbers in increasing order?

A. $\frac{1}{3}, \frac{7}{11}, \frac{4}{7}, \frac{3}{4}$

B. $\frac{1}{3}, \frac{4}{7}, \frac{7}{11}, \frac{3}{4}$

C. $\frac{4}{7}, \frac{3}{4}, \frac{7}{11}, \frac{1}{3}$

D. $\frac{7}{11}, \frac{3}{4}, \frac{4}{7}, \frac{1}{3}$

E. None of them above

36) In 1999, the average worker's income increased $3,000 per year starting from $32,000 annual salary. Which equation represents income greater than average? (I = income, x = number of years after 1999)

A. $I > 3,000\,x + 32,000$

B. $I > -3,000\,x + 32,000$

C. $I < -3,000\,x + 32,000$

D. $I < 3,000\,x - 32,000$

E. $I < 34,000\,x + 32,000$

Questions 37 to 39 are based on the following data

The result of a research shows the number of men and women in four cities of a country.

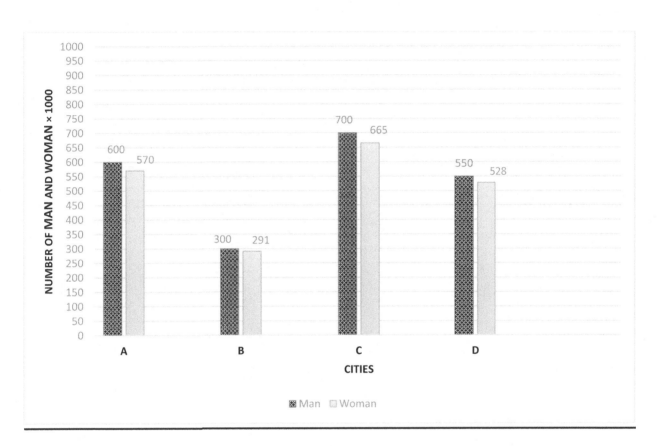

37) What's the ratio of percentage of men in city C to percentage of men in city B?

A. 0.10

C. 0.99

E. 1.00

B. 0.01

D. 1.01

38) What's the minimum ratio of woman to man in the four cities?

A. 0.97

C. 0.95

E. 0.96

B. 0.98

D. 0.99

39) How many women should be added to city D until the ratio of women to men will be 1.3?

A. 122   C. 148   E. 135

B. 187   D. 192

40) What are the values of mode and median in the following set of numbers?

$$3, 2, 7, 5, 7, 7, 3, 3, 3, 7, 2$$

A. Mode: 1, 2 Median: 4   D. Mode: 1, 3 Median: 4

B. Mode: 3, 7 Median: 3   E. Mode: 3, Median: 3

C. Mode: 2, 4 Median: 3

41) x is $y\%$ of what number?

A. $\dfrac{x}{100y}$ C. $\dfrac{100x}{y}$ E. $\dfrac{xy}{100}$

B. $\dfrac{y}{100x}$ D. $\dfrac{100y}{x}$

42) If cotangent of an angel β is 1, then the tangent of angle β is

A. -1 C. 0   E. $-\dfrac{1}{2}$

B. 1   D. $\dfrac{1}{2}$

43) If a box contains red and blue balls in ratio of 4: 5, how many red balls are there if 90 blue balls are in the box?

A. 90   C. 40   E. 8

B. 72   D. 10

44) 6 liters of water are poured into an aquarium that's 20cm long, 5cm wide, and 50cm high. How many cm will the water level in the aquarium rise due to this added water? (1 liter of water = 1,000 cm³)

A. 80   C. 50   E. 4

B. 60   D. 10

45) What is the surface area of the cylinder below?

A. $40\ \pi\ in^2$

B. $40\ \pi^2 in^2$

C. $88\ \pi\ in^2$

D. $88\ \pi^2 in^2$

E. $56\ \pi\ in^2$

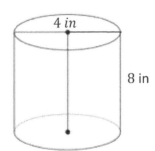

4 in

8 in

46) A chemical solution contains 3% alcohol. If there is 24ml of alcohol, what is the volume of the solution?

A. 320 ml   C. 800 ml   E. 1,400 ml

B. 350 ml   D. 1,200 ml

47) What is the solution of the following inequality?

$$|x - 8| \leq 4$$

A. $x \geq 12 \cup x \leq 8$ D. $x \leq 8$

B. $4 \leq x \leq 12$ E. Set of real numbers

C. $x \geq 12$

48) Which of the following points lies on the line $3x - y = -2$?

A. $(3, -1)$ C. $(-1, -1)$ E. $(0, -3)$

B. $(-1, 3)$ D. $(3, -3)$

49) In the following figure, ABCD is a rectangle, and E and F are points on AD and DC, respectively. The area of ΔBED is 15, and the area of ΔBDF is 20. What is the perimeter of the rectangle?

A. 32

B. 22

C. 20

D. 40

E. 36

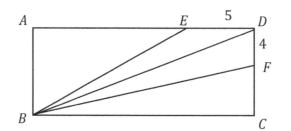

50) In the xy-plane, the point $(5, 7)$ and $(4, 6)$ are on line A. Which of the following equations of lines is parallel to line A?

A. $y = 3x$ C. $y = \frac{x}{2}$ E. $y = x$

B. $y = 10$ D. $y = 2x$

51) When point A $(8, 2)$ is reflected over the y-axis to get the point B, what are the coordinates of point B?

A. $(8, 2)$ C. $(-8, 2)$ E. $(0, 2)$

B. $(-8, -2)$ D. $(8, -2)$

52) A bag contains 16 balls: two green, five black, eight blue, a brown, a red and one white. If 15 balls are removed from the bag at random, what is the probability that a brown ball has been removed?

A. $\frac{1}{3}$

B. $\frac{1}{6}$

C. $\frac{16}{15}$

D. $\frac{15}{16}$

E. $\frac{1}{2}$

53) If a tree casts a 54–foot shadow at the same time that a 5 feet yardstick casts a 3–foot shadow, what is the height of the tree?

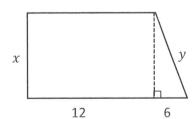

A. 14 ft

B. 30 ft

C. 90 ft

D. 48 ft

E. 52 ft

54) If the area of trapezoid is 120, what is the perimeter of the trapezoid?

A. 37

B. 48

C. 53

D. 57

E. 63

55) If 80% of x equal to 20% of 40, then what is the value of $(x + 4)^2$?

A. 12.20

C. 25.01

E. 196

B. 24

D. 1810

56) If $f(x) = 3x^3 + 6x^2 + 2x$ and $g(x) = -1$, what is the value of $f(g(x))$?

A. 18

C. 14

E. 0

B. 23

D. 1

57) A boat sails 60 miles south and then 25 miles east. How far is the boat from its

start point?

A. 35 miles

C. 80 miles

E. 50 miles

B. 65 miles

D. 100 miles

58) If $x \begin{bmatrix} 2 & 0 \\ 0 & 6 \end{bmatrix} = \begin{bmatrix} x + 3y - 5 & 0 \\ 0 & 8y + 10 \end{bmatrix}$, what is the product of x and y?

A. 1

C. 7

E. 28

B. 4

D. 22

59) If $f(x) = 2^x$ and $g(x) = log_2 x$, which of the following expressions is equal

to $f(2g(p))$?

A. $2P$

C. p^2

E. $\frac{p}{2}$

B. 2^p

D. p^4

60) In the following equation when z is divided by 5, what is the effect on x?

$$x = \frac{8y + \frac{r}{r+1}}{\frac{10}{z}}$$

A. x is divided by 3

B. x is divided by 5

C. x does not change

D. x is multiplied by 5

E. x is multiplied by 3

STOP

This is the End of this Test. You may check your work on this Test if you still have time.

ACT Practice Test 4

Mathematics

❖ **60 Questions.**

❖ **Total time for this test: 60 Minutes**.

❖ **You may use a scientific calculator on this test.**

Administered *Month Year*

1) Convert 640,000 to scientific notation.

    A. 6.40×1000 D. 6.4×10^5

    B. 6.40×10^{-5} E. 6.4×10^4

    C. 6.4×100

2) $(x^4)^{\frac{5}{8}}$ equal to?

    A. $x^{\frac{5}{2}}$ C. $x^{\frac{4}{15}}$ E. $x^{\frac{5}{48}}$

    B. $x^{\frac{53}{8}}$ D. $x^{\frac{8}{53}}$

3) Simplify $\frac{2-5i}{-2i}$?

    A. $\frac{5}{2} + i$ C. $\frac{1}{2} - i$ E. i

    B. $\frac{3}{2} - i$ D. $\frac{1}{2} + i$

4) What is the value of x in the following equation?

$$7^x = 343$$

    A. 4   C. 5   E. 7

    B. 3   D. 6

5) What is the sum of prime numbers between 10 and 20?

    A. 73   C. 70   E. 120

    B. 52   D. 60

6) If $\sqrt{5x} = \sqrt{y}$, then $x =$?

A. $5y$ C. y^2 E. $\frac{y}{5}$

B. $\sqrt{\frac{y}{5}}$ D. $\sqrt{5y}$

7) The average weight of 30 girls in a class is 65 kg and the average weight of 20 boys in the same class is 60 kg. What is the average weight of all the 50 students in that class?

A. 60   C. 61.28   E. 62.48

B. 63   D. 62.90

8) If $y = (-3x^3)^2$, which of the following expressions is equal to y?

A. $-3x^5$ C. $3x^5$ E. $9x^6$

B. $-3x^6$ D. $9x^5$

9) What is the value of the expression $2(x - y) + (1 - x)^2$ when $x = 2$ and $= -3$?

A. -10 C. 11   E. 76

B. -11 D. 32

10) Sophia purchased a sofa for $406.25 The sofa is regularly priced at $625. What was the percent discount Sophia received on the sofa?

A. 1.35%   C. 54%   E. 1.54%

B. 35%   D. 65%

11) If $f(x) = 2x - 5$ and $g(x) = x^2 - 4x$, then find $\left(\frac{f}{g}\right)(x)$.

A. $\dfrac{2x-5}{x^2-4x}$

C. $\dfrac{x-5}{x^2-4}$

E. $\dfrac{x^2-4x}{2x-5}$

B. $\dfrac{x-5}{x^2-4x}$

D. $\dfrac{2x+1}{x^2+4x}$

12) In the standard (x, y) coordinate plane, which of the following lines contains the points $(3, -5)$ and $(8, 10)$?

A. $y = 3x - 14$

D. $y = -\dfrac{1}{3}x + 14$

B. $y = \dfrac{1}{3}x + 14$

E. $y = 3x - 11$

C. $y = -3x + 7$

13) A bank is offering 2.5% simple interest on a savings account. If you deposit $13,000, how much interest will you earn in two years?

A. $450

C. $4,500

E. $4,600

B. $650

D. $6,400

14) If the ratio of home fans to visiting fans in a crowd is 2:4 and all 12,000 seats in a stadium are filled, how many visiting fans are in attendance?

A. 100,000

C. 1,000

E. 8,000

B. 100

D. 10

15) If the interior angles of a quadrilateral are in the ratio 1:3:5:6, what is the measure of the largest angle?

    A. 24°   C. 108°   E. 144°

    B. 72°   D. 120°

16) If $x + sin^2 a + cos^2 a = 4$, then $x = ?$

    A. 1   C. 2   E. 5

    B. 3   D. 4

17) If the area of a circle is 64 square meters, what is its diameter?

    A. 8π C. $\frac{16\sqrt{\pi}}{\pi}$ E. $8\sqrt{\pi}$

    B. $\frac{8}{\pi}$ D. $64\pi^2$

18) The length of a rectangle is $\frac{3}{4}$ times its width. If the width is 32, what is the perimeter of this rectangle?

    A. 38   C. 112   E. 150

    B. 48   D. 169

19) In the figure below, line A is parallel to line B. What is the value of angle x?

    A. 35 degree

    B. 45 degree

    C. 85 degree

    D. 105 degree

    E. 135 degree

20) What is the value of x in the following system of equations?

$$2x + 3y = 8$$
$$6x - 3y = -24$$

A. –2   C. – 1   E. 4

B. 1   D. 3

21) An angle is equal to one fifth of its supplement. What is the measure of that angle?

A. 30   C. 20   E. 45

B. 22.5   D. 44.5

22) Last week 14,000 fans attended a football match. This week three times as many bought tickets, but one sixth of them cancelled their tickets. How many are attending this week?

A. 14,000   C. 70,000   E. 24,000

B. 7,000   D. 35,000

23) If $sin\alpha = \frac{1}{2}$ in a right triangle and the angle α is an acute angle, then what is $cos\,\alpha$?

A. $\frac{3\sqrt{3}}{2}$ C. $\sqrt{3}$ E. $\frac{\sqrt{3}}{2}$

B. $\frac{1}{2}$ D. $\frac{4}{\sqrt{3}}$

24) In following rectangle which statement is true?

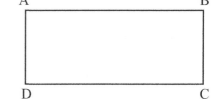

    A. AB is parallel to BC

    B. AB is perpendicular to DC

    C. Length of AB equal to half of length BC

    D. The measure of all the angles equals 360°.

    E. The answer cannot be found from the information given.

25) In the standard (x, y) coordinate system plane, what is the area of the circle with the following equation?

$$(x + 1)^2 + (y - 2)^2 = 4$$

    A. 3π C. 16π E. 2π

    B. 4π D. 9π

26) In two successive years, the population of a town is increased by 25% and 40%. What percent of the population is increased after two years?

    A. 32%   C. 75%   E. 70%

    B. 35%   D. 38%

27) Simplify.

$$6x^2y^3 + 4x^3y^5 - (4x^2y^3 - 3x^3y^5)$$

    A. $-x^2y^3$ C. $7x^2y^3$ E. $6x^5y^8$

    B. $2x^2y^3 - x^3y^5$ D. $7x^3y^5 + 2x^2y^3$

28) What are the zeroes of the function $f(x)=x^3+7x^2+12x$?

A. 0

C. 0, 3, 4

E. 0, − 3, − 4

B. − 3, − 4

D. − 1, − 4

29) If one angle of a right triangle measures 60°, what is the sine of the other acute angle?

A. $\frac{1}{2}$

C. $\frac{\sqrt{3}}{2}$

E. $\sqrt{3}$

B. $\frac{\sqrt{2}}{2}$

D. 1

30) In the following figure, what is the perimeter of $\triangle ABC$ if the area of $\triangle ADC$ is 30?

A. 37.5

B. 21

C. 15

D. 48

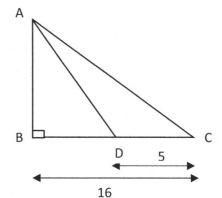

E. The answer cannot be determined from the information given

31) Which of the following is one solution of this equation?

$$2x^2 + 4x - 10 = 0$$

A. $\sqrt{2}+1$

C. $\sqrt{6}-1$

E. $\sqrt{12}$

B. $\sqrt{2}-1$

D. $\sqrt{6}+1$

32) Two-kilograms apple and three-kilograms orange cost \$40.2. If one-kilogram apple costs \$3.6 how much does one-kilogram orange cost?

A. \$11　　　　　　　C. \$5.5　　　　　　　E. \$4

B. \$6　　　　　　　D. \$5

33) Which of the following expressions is equal to $\sqrt{\frac{x^2}{2} + \frac{x^2}{16}}$?

A. x　　　　　　　C. $x\sqrt{x}$　　　　　　　E. $2x$

B. $\frac{3x}{4}$　　　　　　　D. $\frac{x\sqrt{x}}{4}$

Questions 34 to 36 are based on the following data

Number of clothes sold in a clothing store

34) Between which two of the months shown was there a twenty percent increase

in the number of pants sold?

A. January and February   D. April and May

B. February and March   E. May and June

C. March and April

35) During the six-month period shown, what is the mean number of shirts and

median number of shoes per month?

A. 25, 147.5   D. 30, 147.5

B. 149, 25   E. 30, 25

C. 149, 30

36) How many shoes need to be added in April until the ratio of number of pants to number of shoes in April equals to five-twelfth of this ratio in May?

A. 20   C. 25   E. 40

B. 30   D. 35

37) A card is drawn at random from a standard 52–card deck, what is the probability that the card is of hearts? (The deck includes 13 of each suit clubs, diamonds, hearts, and spades)

A. $\frac{1}{3}$ C. $\frac{1}{6}$ E. $\frac{1}{104}$

B. $\frac{1}{4}$ D. $\frac{1}{52}$

38) A football team had $20,000 to spend on supplies. The team spent $14,000 on new balls. New sport shoes cost $120 each. Which of the following inequalities represent how many new shoes the team can purchase?

A. $120x + 14,000 \le 20,000$ D. $14,000x + 120 \ge 20,000$

B. $120x + 14,000 \ge 20,000$ E. $14,000x + 1,200 \ge 20,000$

C. $24,000x + 140 \le 30,000$

39) If $x = 6$, what is the value of y in the following equation?

$$4y = \frac{2x^2}{3} + 8$$

A. 8   C. 60   E. 150

B. 35   D. 16

40) A swimming pool holds 3,600 cubic feet of water. The swimming pool is 12 feet long and 10 feet wide. How deep is the swimming pool?

A. 6 feet   C. 12 feet   E. 30 feet

B. 4 feet   D. 15 feet

41) The ratio of boys to girls in a school is 2:6. If there are 400 students in a school, how many boys are in the school.

A. 240   C. 400   E. 100

B. 500   D. 300

42) If $(x - 3)^2 + 1 > 3x + 1$, then x can equal which of the following?

A. 2   C. 8   E. 4

B. 6   D. 3

43) Let r and p be constants. If $x^2 + 6x + r$ factors into $(x + 5)(x + p)$, the values of r and p respectively are?

A. 5, 1   C. 2, 5

B. 1, 5   D. 5, 2

E. The answer cannot be found from the information given.

44) If 150% of a number is 75, then what is 60% of that number?

A. 45   C. 48   E. 80

B. 50   D. 55

45) The width of a box is one third of its length. The height of the box is one third of its width. If the length of the box is 45 cm, what is the volume of the box?

A. 144 cm³

B. 324 cm³

C. 576 cm³

D. 3,375 cm³

E. 2,105 cm³

46) The average of five consecutive numbers is 34. What is the smallest number?

A. 28

B. 34

C. 32

D. 12

E. 8

47) The surface area of a cylinder is $132\pi\ cm^2$. If its height is 5 cm, what is the radius of the cylinder?

A. 13 cm

B. 11 cm

C. 12 cm

D. 6 cm

E. 7 cm

48) In a coordinate plane, triangle ABC has coordinates: $(4,-2)$, $(-2,-3)$, and $(3,5)$. If triangle ABC is reflected over the y-axis, what are the coordinates of the new image?

A. $(4,-2),(-2,-3),(3,5)$

B. $(-2,4),(-3,-2),(5,3)$

C. $(-4,-2),(2,-3),(-3,5)$

D. $(4,-2),(-2,3),(3,-5)$

E. $(-2,-4),(3,2),(-5,-3)$

49) What is the slope of a line that is perpendicular to the line $9x - 3y = 18$?

A. -3

B. $-\frac{1}{3}$

C. 4

D. 12

E. 14

50) What is the difference in area between a 9 cm by 5 cm rectangle and a circle with diameter of 16 cm? ($\pi = 3$)

A. 47

B. 147

C. 9

D. 6

E. 3

51) If $f(x) = 4x^3 + 4$ and $g(x) = \frac{1}{x}$, what is the value of $f(g(x))$?

A. $\frac{1}{4x^3 + 4}$

B. $\frac{4}{x^3}$

C. $\frac{1}{4x}$

D. $\frac{1}{4x + 4}$

E. $\frac{4}{x^3} + 4$

52) A cruise line ship left Port A and traveled 50 miles due west and then 120 miles due north. At this point, what is the shortest distance from the cruise to port A?

A. 70 miles

B. 80 miles

C. 150 miles

D. 130 miles

E. 230 miles

53) The length of a rectangle is 2 meters greater than 3 times its width. The perimeter of the rectangle is 36 meters. What is the area of the rectangle?

A. 16 m²

B. 36 m²

C. 56 m²

D. 72 m²

E. 110 m²

54) Tickets to a movie cost $12.50 for adults and $6.50 for students. A group of 16 friends purchased tickets for $128. How many student tickets did they buy?

A. 4   C. 6   E. 8

B. 12   D. 10

55) What is the solution of the following inequality?

$$|x - 3| \geq 5$$

A. $x \geq 8 \ \cup \ x \leq -2$ D. $x \leq -2$

B. $-2 \leq x \leq 8$ E. Set of real numbers

C. $x \geq 8$

56) If $\tan x = \frac{5}{12}$, then $\sin x =$

A. $\frac{1}{2}$ C. $\frac{12}{13}$

B. $\frac{5}{13}$ D. $\frac{7}{12}$

E. It cannot be determined from the information given.

57) In the following figure, ABCD is a rectangle. If $a = \sqrt{3}$, and $b = 4a$, find the area of the shaded region. (the shaded region is a trapezoid)

A. 12

B. 20

C. $10\sqrt{3}$

D. $20\sqrt{3}$

E. $12\sqrt{3}$

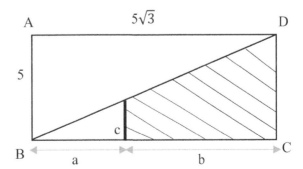

58) If the ratio of $7a$ to $3b$ is $\frac{1}{15}$, what is the ratio of a to b?

A. 15

C. $\frac{1}{35}$

E. $\frac{1}{15}$

B. 35

D. $\frac{1}{30}$

59) If $A = \begin{bmatrix} -1 & 3 \\ 1 & -3 \end{bmatrix}$ and $B = \begin{bmatrix} 5 & 1 \\ -3 & 4 \end{bmatrix}$, then $2A - B =$

A. $\begin{bmatrix} -4 & 1 \\ 3 & -5 \end{bmatrix}$

C. $\begin{bmatrix} 2 & 3 \\ -1 & 1 \end{bmatrix}$

E. $\begin{bmatrix} -7 & 5 \\ 5 & -10 \end{bmatrix}$

B. $\begin{bmatrix} -2 & 4 \\ 2 & -4 \end{bmatrix}$

D. $\begin{bmatrix} 1 & 5 \\ 0 & -1 \end{bmatrix}$

60) What is the amplitude of the graph of the equation $y - 1 = 3cos2x$? (half the

distance between the graph's minimum and maximum y-values in standard (x,

y) coordinate plane is the amplitude of a graph.)

A. 6

C. 2

E. 0.5

B. 3

D. 1

STOP

This is the End of this Test. You may check your work on this Test if you still have time.

ACT Practice Test 5

Mathematics

❖ **60 Questions.**

❖ **Total time for this test: 60 Minutes**.

❖ **You may use a scientific calculator on this test.**

Administered *Month Year*

1) $5^{\frac{5}{2}} \times 5^{\frac{1}{2}} = ?$

    A. 5^5

    B. 5^4

    C. 5^3

    D. 5^6

    E. 5^0

2) If $\frac{5x}{36} = \frac{x-2}{6}$, $x = ?$

    A. $\frac{1}{12}$

    B. $\frac{3}{5}$

    C. 6

    D. 12

    E. $\frac{12}{5}$

3) 121 is equal to?

    A. $25 - (5 \times 8) + (7 \times 20)$

    B. $\left(\frac{10}{7} \times 63\right) + \left(\frac{124}{4}\right)$

    C. $\left(\left(\frac{70}{6} + \frac{22}{3}\right) \times 7\right) - \frac{20}{3} + \frac{130}{6}$

    D. $(3 \times 11) + (42 \times 2.5) - 14$

    E. $\frac{148}{8} + \frac{207}{2}$

4) Five years ago, Amy was three times as old as Mike was. If Mike is 11 years old now, how old is Amy?

    A. 33

    B. 25

    C. 16

    D. 21

    E. 23

5) A number is chosen at random from 1 to 15. Find the probability of not selecting

a composite number.

A. $\dfrac{3}{15}$ 　　　　C. $\dfrac{2}{5}$ 　　　　E. 1

B. 15 　　　　D. 2

6) If $|a| < 3$ then which of the following is true? $(b > 0)$?

VII. $-3b < ba < 3b$

VIII. $-a < a^2 < a \quad if \ a < 0$

IX. $-13 < 3a - 4 < 5$

A. I only 　　　　C. I and III only 　　　　E. I, II and III

B. II only 　　　　D. III only

7) Removing which of the following numbers will change the average of the

numbers to 7?

$$2, 5, 6, 9, 12, 13$$

A. 12 　　　　C. 6 　　　　E. 13

B. 5 　　　　D. 2

8) A rope weighs 800 grams per meter of length. What is the weight in kilograms

of 15.5 meters of this rope? (1 kilograms = 1,000 grams)

A. 0.0124 　　　　C. 124 　　　　E. 12,400

B. 0.124 　　　　D. 1,240

9) If $y = 2ab + 5b^2$, what is y when $a = 4$ and $b = 2$?

A. 26　　　　　　　C. 20　　　　　　　E. 36

B. 16　　　　　　　D. 18

10) If $f(x) = 2 + 3x$ and $g(x) = -2x^2 - 6 - x$, then find $(g - f)(x)$?

A. $2x^2 - 4x - 8$　　　C. $-2x^2 - 4x + 8$　　　E. $-2x^2 + 4x - 8$

B. $2x^2 - 4x + 8$　　　D. $-2x^2 - 4x - 8$

11) The marked price of a computer is D dollar. Its price decreased by 70% in January and later increased by 15 % in February. What is the final price of the computer in D dollar?

A. 3.45 D　　　　　　C. 0.75 D　　　　　　E. 1.30 D

B. 34.5 D　　　　　　D. 7.50 D

12) The number 64.7 is 100 times greater than which of the following numbers?

A. 0.0647　　　　　　C. 0.00647　　　　　　E. 64.700

B. 0.647　　　　　　D. 6.470

13) David's current age is 70 years, and Ava's current age is 10 years. In how many years David's age will be 5 times Ava's age?

A. 5　　　　　　　　C. 9　　　　　　　　E. 15

B. 7　　　　　　　　D. 12

14) How many tiles of 11 cm² is needed to cover a floor of dimension 7 cm by 33 cm?

    A. 16   C. 25   E. 26

    B. 19   D. 21

15) What is the median of these numbers? 24, 9, 19, 32, 11, 15, 5

    A. 15   C. 19   E. 32

    B. 9   D. 11

16) A company pays its employer \$8,000 plus 6% of all sales profit. If x is the number of all sales profit, which of the following represents the employer's revenue?

    A. $0.06x$ C. $0.06x + 8,000$ E. $-0.94x - 8,000$

    B. $0.94x - 8,000$ D. $0.94x + 8,000$

17) What is the area of a square whose diagonal is 6 cm?

    A. 36 cm²   C. 24 cm²   E. 218 cm²

    B. 18 cm²   D. 12 cm²

18) What is the value of x in the following figure?

    A. 125

    B. 175

    C. 55

    D. 155

    E. 105

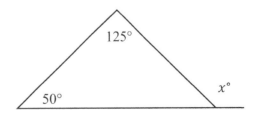

19) Right triangle ABC is shown below. Which of the following is true for all possible values of angle A and B?

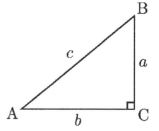

A. $\cot A = \cot B$

B. $\tan^2 A = \tan^2 B$

C. $\cot A = 1$

D. $\cos A = \sin B$

E. $\cot A = \cos B$

20) What is the value of y in the following system of equation?

$$2x - 5y = -8$$

$$-x + 2y = 3$$

A. -5

B. -3

C. 3

D. 6

E. 2

21) How long does a 312–miles trip take moving at 60 miles per hour (mph)?

A. 5 hours

B. 5 hours and 36 minutes

C. 5 hours and 18 minutes

D. 6 hours and 24 minutes

E. 12 hours and 45 minutes

22) From the figure, which of the following must be true? (figure not drawn to scale)

A. $y = 2z$

B. $y = 7x$

C. $y \geq x$

D. $y + 6x = z$

E. $z > x$

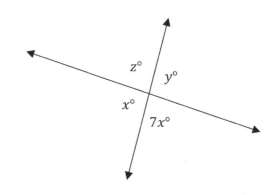

23) Which is the correct statement?

A. $\frac{1}{5} < 0.16$

B. $20\% = \frac{4}{5}$

C. $4 < \frac{7}{3}$

D. $\frac{5}{8} > 0.59$

E. None of them above

24) When 30% of 70 is added to 18% of 500, the resulting number is:

A. 21

B. 90

C. 111

D. 121

E. 189

25) A ladder leans against a wall forming a 60° angle between the ground and the ladder. If the bottom of the ladder is 30 feet away from the wall, how long is the ladder?

A. 40 feet

B. 80 feet

C. 50 feet

D. 60 feet

E. 160 feet

26) If 75% of a class are girls, and 12% of girls play tennis, what percent of the class play tennis?

A. 9%

B. 10%

C. 12%

D. 18%

E. 24%

27) If x is a real number, and if $x^3 + 52 = 170$, then x lies between which two consecutive integers?

A. 1 and 2

B. 2 and 3

C. 3 and 4

D. 4 and 5

E. 5 and 6

28) If $(x-5)^2 = 9$ which of the following could be the value of $(x-6)(x-5)$?

A. 2   C. 7   E. −5

B. 6   D. −2

29) Simplify.

$$4x^2 + 5y^5 - 2x^2 + 5z^3 - y^2 + 4x^3 - 2y^5 + 3z^3$$

A. $2x^2 - 4y^2 + 3y^5 + 8z^3$

B. $2x^2 + 4x^3 - y^2 + 3y^5 + 8z^3$

C. $2x^2 + 4x^3 + 3y^5 + 8z^3$

D. $2x^2 - 4x^3 - 2y^2 + y^5 + 8z^3$

E. $2x^2 + 4x^3 - 3y^2 + 8z^3$

30) In four successive hours, a car travels 44 km, 46 km, 42 km and 52 km. In the next four hours, it travels with an average speed of 55 km per hour. Find the total distance the car traveled in 8 hours.

A. 404 km   C. 220 km   E. 1,440 km

B. 184 km   D. 808 km

31) From last year, the price of gasoline has increased from $2.04 per gallon to $3.06 per gallon. The new price is what percent of the original price?

A. 52%   C. 130%   E. 130%

B. 150%   D. 170%

32) Simplify $(-2 + 3i)(5 + 6i)$,

A. $28 - 3i$

B. $8 - 3i$

C. $-10 + 3i$

D. $-28 + 3i$

E. $3i$

33) If $\tan \theta = \frac{5}{12}$ and $\sin \theta > 0$, then $\cos \theta = ?$

A. $-\frac{5}{12}$

B. $\frac{12}{13}$

C. $\frac{5}{13}$

D. $-\frac{13}{5}$

E. 1

34) Which of the following has the half period and five times the amplitude of graph $y = sinx$?

A. $y = \frac{1}{2} \sin 5x$

B. $y = 5\sin \left(\frac{x}{2} + 5\right)$

C. $y = 2.5 \sin 2x$

D. $y = 5 + 5 \sin 2x$

E. $y = 4 + \sin \frac{x}{2}$

35) Which of the following shows the numbers in increasing order?

A. $\frac{1}{2}, \frac{8}{13}, \frac{5}{7}, \frac{2}{5}$

B. $\frac{2}{5}, \frac{1}{2}, \frac{8}{13}, \frac{5}{7}$

C. $\frac{5}{7}, \frac{2}{5}, \frac{8}{13}, \frac{1}{2}$

D. $\frac{2}{5}, \frac{7}{11}, \frac{5}{7}, \frac{1}{2}$

E. None of them above

36) In 1999, the average worker's income increased $4,000 per year starting from $36,000 annual salary. Which equation represents income greater than average? (I = income, x = number of years after 1999)

A. $I > 4,000\ x + 36,000$

B. $I > -4,000\ x + 36,000$

C. $I < -4,000\ x + 36,000$

D. $I < 4,000\ x - 36,000$

E. $I < 36,000\ x + 4,000$

Questions 37 to 39 are based on the following data

The result of a research shows the number of men and women in four cities of a country.

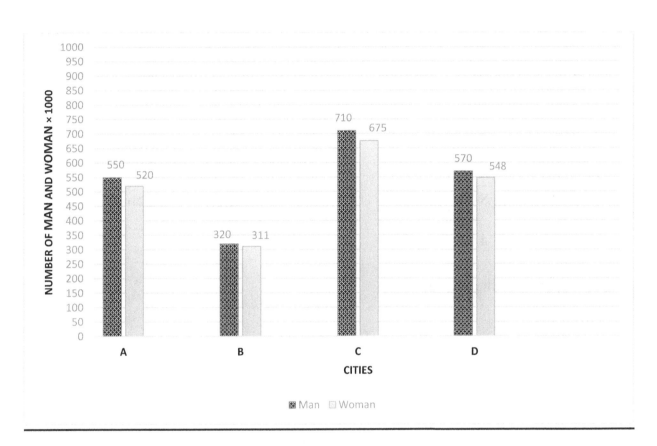

37) What's the ratio of percentage of men in city C to percentage of men in city B?

A. 0.11   C. 0.99   E. 1.11

B. 9.991   D. 99.11

38) What's the minimum ratio of woman to man in the four cities?

A. 0.97   C. 0.95   E. 0.96

B. 0.98   D. 0.99

39) How many women should be added to city D until the ratio of women to men will be 1.4?

    A. 222   C. 128   E. 138

    B. 228   D. 298

40) What are the values of mode and median in the following set of numbers?

$$5, 4, 8, 6, 8, 8, 5, 5, 5, 8, 4$$

    A. Mode: 5, 4 Median: 4   D. Mode: 3, 5 Median: 4

    B. Mode: 5, 8 Median: 5   E. Mode: 5, Median: 5

    C. Mode: 2, 4 Median: 5

41) y is $x\%$ of what number?

    A. $\dfrac{y}{100x}$ C. $\dfrac{100y}{x}$ E. $\dfrac{xy}{100}$

    B. $\dfrac{x}{100y}$ D. $\dfrac{100x}{y}$

42) If cotangent of an angel β is $\sqrt{2}$, then the tangent of angle β is

    A. -1 C. $\sqrt{2}$ E. $-\dfrac{\sqrt{2}}{2}$

    B. 1   D. $\dfrac{\sqrt{2}}{2}$

43) If a box contains red and blue balls in ratio of 3: 8, how many red balls are there if 96 blue balls are in the box?

    A. 45   C. 30   E. 11

    B. 36   D. 20

44) 8 liters of water are poured into an aquarium that's 40cm long, 2cm wide, and 60cm high. How many cm will the water level in the aquarium rise due to this added water? (1 liter of water = 1,000 cm^3)

A. 90　　　　　　　C. 40　　　　　　　E. 8

B. 100　　　　　　D. 20

45) What is the surface area of the cylinder below?

A. 78 π in^2

B. 87 π^2 in^2

C. 98 π in^2

D. 86 π^2 in^2

E. 606 π in^2

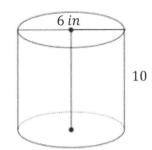

6 in

10

46) A chemical solution contains 4% alcohol. If there is 28ml of alcohol, what is the volume of the solution?

A. 350 ml　　　　　C. 700 ml　　　　　E. 1,200 ml

B. 450 ml　　　　　D. 1,100 ml

47) What is the solution of the following inequality?

$$|x - 5| \leq 2$$

A. $x \geq 7 \cup x \leq 3$　　　　　　D. $x \leq 7$

B. $3 \leq x \leq 7$　　　　　　　　　E. Set of real numbers

C. $x \geq 10$

48) Which of the following points lies on the line $2x - 3y = 5$?

    A. $(1, -2)$ C. $(-2, -3)$ E. $(0, -2)$

    B. $(-3, 0)$ D. $(1, -4)$

49) In the following figure, ABCD is a rectangle, and E and F are points on AD and DC, respectively. The area of ΔBED is 18, and the area of ΔBDF is 10. What is the perimeter of the rectangle?

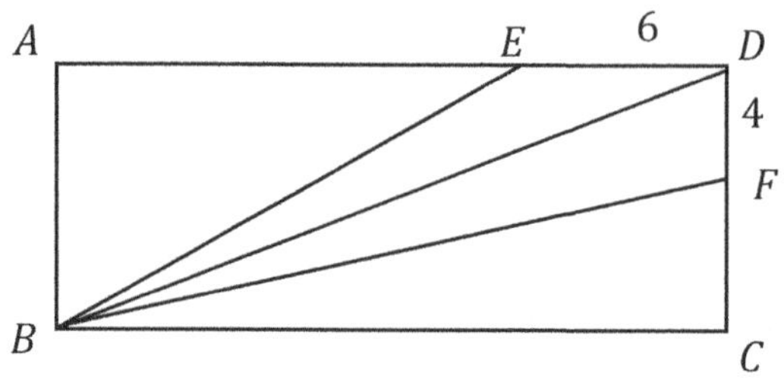

    A. 32

    B. 24

    C. 18

    D. 56

    E. 48

50) In the xy-plane, the point $(3, 9)$ and $(2, 8)$ are on line A. Which of the following equations of lines is parallel to line A?

    A. $y = 2x$ C. $y = \frac{x}{3}$ E. $y = x$

    B. $y = 8$ D. $y = -x$

51) When point A $(7, 3)$ is reflected over the y-axis to get the point B, what are the coordinates of point B?

    A. $(7, 3)$ C. $(-7, 3)$ E. $(0, 3)$

    B. $(-7, -3)$ D. $(7, -3)$

52) A bag contains 18 balls: three green, four black, six blue, a brown, two red and two white. If 17 balls are removed from the bag at random, what is the probability that a brown ball has been removed?

A. $\frac{1}{2}$

B. $\frac{1}{8}$

C. $\frac{18}{17}$

D. $\frac{1}{18}$

E. $\frac{17}{18}$

53) If a tree casts a 48–foot shadow at the same time that a 7 feet yardstick casts a 6–foot shadow, what is the height of the tree?

A. 13 ft

B. 52 ft

C. 56 ft

D. 48 ft

E. 42 ft

54) If the area of trapezoid is 210, what is the perimeter of the trapezoid?

A. 27

B. 62

C. 54

D. 58

E. 64

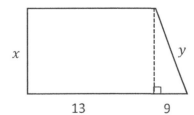

55) If 60% of x equal to 30% of 30, then what is the value of $(x+3)^2$?

    A. 18.20   C. 32.04   E. 324

    B. 32   D. 3,240

56) If $f(x) = 2x^3 + 3x^2 + x$ and $g(x) = -2$, what is the value of $f(g(x))$?

    A. 6   C. 16   E. 7

    B. 2   D. −6

57) A boat sails 36 miles south and then 15 miles east. How far is the boat from its

    start point?

    A. 36 miles   C. 88 miles   E. 51 miles

    B. 39 miles   D. 38 miles

58) If $x \begin{bmatrix} 3 & 0 \\ 0 & 4 \end{bmatrix} = \begin{bmatrix} 2x+y-5 & 0 \\ 0 & 3y-12 \end{bmatrix}$, what is the product of x and y?

    A. 3   C. 8   E. 24

    B. 12   D. 20

59) If $f(x) = 5^x$ and $g(x) = log_5 x$, which of the following expressions is equal

    to $f(5g(p))$?

    A. $5P$ C. p^5 E. $\frac{p}{5}$

    B. 5^p D. $5p^5$

60) In the following equation when z is divided by 6, what is the effect on x?

$$x = \frac{7y + \frac{r}{2r+3}}{\frac{12}{z}}$$

A. x is divided by 2

D. x is multiplied by 6

B. x is divided by 6

E. x is multiplied by 2

C. x does not change

STOP

This is the End of this Test. You may check your work on this Test if you still have time.

ACT Practice Test 6

Mathematics

❖ **60 Questions.**

❖ **Total time for this test: 60 Minutes**.

❖ **You may use a scientific calculator on this test.**

Administered *Month Year*

1) Convert 7,800,000 to scientific notation.

    A. $7.80 \times 1,000$ D. 7.8×10^6

    B. 7.80×10^{-6} E. 7.8×10^5

    C. 7.8×100

2) $(x^3)^{\frac{4}{9}}$ equal to?

    A. $x^{\frac{4}{3}}$ C. $x^{\frac{4}{12}}$ E. $x^{\frac{4}{18}}$

    B. $x^{\frac{7}{9}}$ D. $x^{\frac{9}{13}}$

3) Simplify $\frac{3-4i}{-3i}$?

    A. $\frac{4}{3}+i$ C. $\frac{1}{3}-i$ E. $3i$

    B. $\frac{4}{3}-i$ D. $\frac{1}{3}+i$

4) What is the value of x in the following equation?

$$8^x = 512$$

    A. 8   C. 8   E. 2

    B. 3   D. 9

5) What is the sum of prime numbers between 1 and 10?

    A. 4   C. 15   E. 18

    B. 10   D. 17

6) If $\sqrt{7x} = \sqrt{y}$, then $x =$?

A. $7y$

C. y^2

E. $\frac{y}{7}$

B. $\sqrt{\frac{y}{7}}$

D. $\sqrt{7y}$

7) The average weight of 24 girls in a class is 50 kg and the average weight of 26 boys in the same class is 55 kg. What is the average weight of all the 50 students in that class?

A. 56

C. 62.28

E. 52

B. 52.6

D. 62.60

8) If $y = (-2x^4)^3$, which of the following expressions is equal to y?

A. $-2x^4$

C. $8x^5$

E. $-8x^{12}$

B. $-2x^7$

D. $8x^7$

9) What is the value of the expression $4(x + y) + (2 - x)^2$ when $x = 3$ and $y = -1$?

A. $- 12$

C. 9

E. 16

B. -21

D. -9

10) Sophia purchased a sofa for $235.80 The sofa is regularly priced at $524. What was the percent discount Sophia received on the sofa?

A. 1.65%

C. 55%

E. 1.45%

B. 65%

D. 45%

11) If $f(x) = 3x - 8$ and $g(x) = 2x^2 - 5x$, then find $(\frac{f}{g})(x)$.

A. $\frac{3x-8}{2x^2-5x}$

C. $\frac{x-5}{x^2-4}$

E. $\frac{x^2-4x}{3x-8}$

B. $\frac{x-8}{2x^2-5x}$

D. $\frac{3x+8}{x^2+5x}$

12) In the standard (x, y) coordinate plane, which of the following lines contains the points $(1, -7)$ and $(6, 8)$?

A. $y = 3x - 10$

D. $y = -\frac{1}{3}x + 10$

B. $y = \frac{1}{3}x + 10$

E. $y = 3x - 7$

C. $y = -3x + 7$

13) A bank is offering 1.5% simple interest on a savings account. If you deposit $15,000, how much interest will you earn in three years?

A. $650

C. $6,500

E. $6,600

B. $675

D. $6,700

14) If the ratio of home fans to visiting fans in a crowd is $3 : 5$ and all 16,000 seats in a stadium are filled, how many visiting fans are in attendance?

A. 100,000

C. 9,000

E. 10,000

B. 1,000

D. 10

15) If the interior angles of a quadrilateral are in the ratio 1:3:7:9, what is the measure of the largest angle?

    A. 54°   C. 198°   E. 162°

    B. 18°   D. 126°

16) If $x + 2sin^2 a + 2cos^2 a = 6$, then $x =$?

    A. 2   C. 3   E. 7

    B. 4   D. 6

17) If the area of a circle is 100 square meters, what is its diameter?

    A. 10π C. $\frac{20\sqrt{\pi}}{\pi}$ E. $10\sqrt{\pi}$

    B. $\frac{10}{\pi}$ D. $100\pi^2$

18) The length of a rectangle is $\frac{4}{5}$ times its width. If the width is 40, what is the perimeter of this rectangle?

    A. 32   C. 144   E. 154

    B. 45   D. 121

19) In the figure below, line A is parallel to line B. What is the value of angle x?

    A. 55 degree

    B. 65 degree

    C. 95 degree

    D. 115 degree

    E. 125 degree

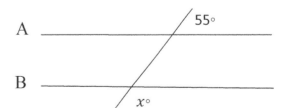

20) What is the value of x in the following system of equations?

$$x + 2y = 7$$
$$4x + 5y = 22$$

A. 3   C. -3 E. 6

B. 2   D. 5

21) An angle is equal to one fourth of its supplement. What is the measure of that

angle?

A. 36   C. 30   E. 60

B. 26.5   D. 45

22) Last week 15,000 fans attended a football match. This week two times as many

bought tickets, but one fifth of them cancelled their tickets. How many are

attending this week?

A. 15,000   C. 60,000   E. 30,000

B. 6,000   D. 24,000

23) If $sin\alpha = \frac{\sqrt{3}}{2}$ in a right triangle and the angle α is an acute angle, then what is

$cos\ \alpha$?

A. $\frac{\sqrt{3}}{3}$ C. $\sqrt{3}$ E. $\frac{1}{2}$

B. $\frac{1}{3}$ D. $\frac{1}{\sqrt{3}}$

24) In following squares which statement is true?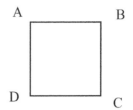

    A. AB is parallel to BC

    B. AB is perpendicular to DC

    C. Length of AB equal to half of length BC

    D. The measure of all the angles equals 360°.

    E. The answer cannot be found from the information given.

25) In the standard (x, y) coordinate system plane, what is the area of the circle with the following equation?

$$(x + 2)^2 + (y - 1)^2 = 9$$

    A. 2π C. 18π E. 3π

    B. 9π D. 6π

26) In two successive years, the population of a town is increased by 15% and 30%. What percent of the population is increased after two years?

    A. 30%   C. 49.5%   E. 55.5%

    B. 45%   D. 35.5%

27) Simplify.

$$8x^5y^2 + 3x^3y^4 - (2x^5y^2 - 4x^3y^4)$$

    A. $-x^5y^3$ C. $8x^2y^3$ E. $8x^5y^6$

    B. $6x^5y^3 - 7x^5y^5$ D. $6x^5y^2 + 7x^3y^4$

28) What are the zeroes of the function $f(x) = 2x^3 + 14x^2 + 20x$?

A. 0

C. $0, 2, 4$

E. $0, -2, -5$

B. $-2, 4$

D. $-2, -3$

29) If one angle of a right triangle measures $30°$, what is the sine of the other acute angle?

A. $\frac{\sqrt{3}}{2}$

C. $\frac{1}{2}$

E. $\sqrt{2}$

B. $\frac{\sqrt{2}}{2}$

D. 1

30) In the following figure, what is the perimeter of $\Delta\ ABC$ if the area of $\Delta\ ADC$ is 45?

A. 57.5

B. 26

C. 25

D. 60

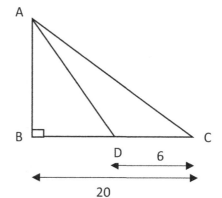

E. The answer cannot be determined from the information given

31) Which of the following is one solution of this equation?

$$3x^2 + 5x - 8 = 0$$

A. $\sqrt{5} + 1$

C. 1

E. $\sqrt{15}$

B. $\sqrt{5} - 1$

D. $\sqrt{5}$

32) Three-kilograms apple and four-kilograms orange cost $51.2. If one-kilogram apple costs $2.4 how much does one-kilogram orange cost?

A. $11

B. $8

C. $6.5

D. $7

E. $12

33) Which of the following expressions is equal to $\sqrt{\dfrac{3x^2}{5} + \dfrac{x^2}{25}}$?

A. $5x$

B. $\dfrac{4x}{5}$

C. $2x\sqrt{x}$

D. $\dfrac{x\sqrt{x}}{5}$

E. $4x$

Questions 34 to 36 are based on the following data

Number of clothes sold in a clothing store

34) Between which two of the months shown was there a twenty percent increase in the number of pants sold?

A. January and February

B. February and March

C. March and April

D. April and May

E. May and June

35) During the six-month period shown, what is the mean number of shirts and median number of shoes per month?

A. 30, 137.5

B. 149, 25

C. 139, 25

D. 30, 139

E. 30, 25

36) How many shoes need to be added in February until the ratio of number of pants to number of shoes in February equals to seven-eighth of this ratio in March?

   A. 2   C. 5   E. 20

   B. 9   D. 18

37) A card is drawn at random from a standard 52–card deck, what is the probability that the card is of hearts or diamonds? (The deck includes 13 of each suit clubs, diamonds, hearts, and spades)

   A. $\frac{1}{5}$ C. $\frac{1}{13}$ E. $\frac{1}{52}$

   B. $\frac{1}{2}$ D. $\frac{1}{26}$

38) A football team had \$25,000 to spend on supplies. The team spent \$18,000 on new balls. New sport shoes cost \$110 each. Which of the following inequalities represent how many new shoes the team can purchase?

   A. $110x + 18{,}000 \le 25{,}000$ D. $18{,}000x + 110 \ge 25{,}000$

   B. $110x + 18{,}000 \ge 25{,}000$ E. $18{,}000x + 25{,}000 \ge 110$

   C. $25{,}000x + 110 \le 18{,}000$

39) If $x = 4$, what is the value of y in the following equation? $5y = \frac{3x^2}{8} + 9$

   A. 3   C. 65   E. 120

   B. 15   D. 12

40) A swimming pool holds 4,800 cubic feet of water. The swimming pool is 15 feet long and 8 feet wide. How deep is the swimming pool?

A. 8 feet   C. 15 feet   E. 40 feet

B. 23 feet   D. 25 feet

41) The ratio of boys to girls in a school is 3:7. If there are 320 students in a school, how many boys are in the school.

A. 80   C. 320   E. 96

B. 600   D. 116

42) If $(x - 2)^2 + 3 > 2x + 3$, then x can equal which of the following?

A. 1   C. 7   E. 3

B. 5   D. 2

43) Let r and p be constants. If $x^2 + 4x + r$ factors into $(x + 3)(x + p)$, the values of r and p respectively are?

A. 3, 1   C. 2, 3

B. 1, 3   D. 3, 2

E. The answer cannot be found from the information given.

44) If 140% of a number is 70, then what is 80% of that number?

A. 35   C. 40   E. 70

B. 60   D. 45

45) The width of a box is half of its length. The height of the box is half of its width. If the length of the box is 20 cm, what is the volume of the box?

A. 200 cm³   D. 1,000 cm³

B. 100 cm³   E. 10,000 cm³

C. 2,000 cm³

46) The average of six consecutive numbers is 24. What is the smallest number?

A. 25   D. 15.5

B. 30.5   E. 15

C. 21.5

47) The surface area of a cylinder is $120\pi \ cm^2$. If its height is 7 cm, what is the radius of the cylinder?

A. 18 cm   D. 5 cm

B. 10 cm   E. 4 cm

C. 12 cm

48) In a coordinate plane, triangle ABC has coordinates: $(5, -1)$, $(-4, -2)$, and $(2, 4)$. If triangle ABC is reflected over the y-axis, what are the coordinates of the new image?

A. $(5, -1), (-2, -4), (4, 2)$ D. $(4, -2), (-2, 4), (5, -2)$

B. $(-2, 4), (-4, -2), (5, -1)$ E. $(-4, -2), (2, 4), (-5, -1)$

C. $(-5, -1), (4, -2), (-2, 4)$

49) What is the slope of a line that is perpendicular to the line $8x - 2y = 16$?

A. -4　　　　　　　　C. 6　　　　　　　　E. 16

B. $-\frac{1}{4}$　　　　　　　　D. 8

50) What is the difference in area between a 8 cm by 4 cm rectangle and a circle

with diameter of 12 cm? ($\pi = 3$)

A. 46　　　　　　　　C. 32　　　　　　　　E. 12

B. 76　　　　　　　　D. 108

51) If $f(x) = 3x^3 + 5$ and $g(x) = \frac{2}{x}$, what is the value of $f(g(x))$?

A. $\frac{8}{5x^3 + 5}$　　　　　　C. $\frac{6}{5x}$　　　　　　E. $\frac{32}{x^3} + 5$

B. $\frac{5}{x^3}$　　　　　　D. $\frac{1}{5x + 5}$

52) A cruise line ship left Port A and traveled 21 miles due west and then 28 miles

due north. At this point, what is the shortest distance from the cruise to port A?

A. 50 miles　　　　　　C. 30 miles　　　　　　E. 49 miles

B. 40 miles　　　　　　D. 35 miles

53) The length of a rectangle is 5 meters greater than 7 times its width. The

perimeter of the rectangle is 90 meters. What is the area of the rectangle?

A. 45 m^2　　　　　　C. 200 m^2　　　　　　E. 180 m^2

B. 300 m^2　　　　　　D. 90 m^2

54) Tickets to a movie cost $10.50 for adults and $5.50 for students. A group of 18 friends purchased tickets for $119. How many student tickets did they buy?

A. 4   C. 11   E. 7

B. 14   D. 18

55) What is the solution of the following inequality?

$$|x - 4| \geq 7$$

A. $x \geq 11 \cup x \leq -3$ D. $x \leq -3$

B. $-3 \leq x \leq 11$ E. Set of real numbers

C. $x \geq 11$

56) If $\tan x = \frac{15}{20}$, then $\sin x =$

A. $\frac{1}{5}$ C. $\frac{12}{25}$

B. $\frac{15}{25}$ D. $\frac{7}{25}$

E. It cannot be determined from the information given.

57) In the following figure, ABCD is a rectangle. If $a = \sqrt{2}$, and $b = 2a$, find the area of the shaded region. (the shaded region is a trapezoid)

A. 15

B. 10

C. $12\sqrt{2}$

D. $8\sqrt{2}$

E. $4\sqrt{2}$

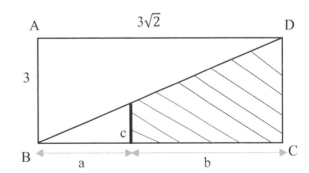

58) If the ratio of $9a$ to $8b$ is $\frac{1}{16}$, what is the ratio of a to b?

A. 16

B. 18

C. $\frac{1}{18}$

D. $\frac{1}{32}$

E. $\frac{1}{16}$

59) If $A = \begin{bmatrix} 1 & 1 \\ 2 & -1 \end{bmatrix}$ and $B = \begin{bmatrix} 4 & 2 \\ -2 & 3 \end{bmatrix}$, then $3A - B =$

A. $\begin{bmatrix} -3 & 1 \\ 4 & -4 \end{bmatrix}$

B. $\begin{bmatrix} -7 & 1 \\ 2 & -6 \end{bmatrix}$

C. $\begin{bmatrix} 4 & 2 \\ -1 & 3 \end{bmatrix}$

D. $\begin{bmatrix} 1 & 5 \\ 0 & -1 \end{bmatrix}$

E. $\begin{bmatrix} -7 & 1 \\ 8 & -6 \end{bmatrix}$

60) What is the amplitude of the graph of the equation $y - 2 = 5cos2x$? (half the distance between the graph's minimum and maximum y-values in standard (x, y) coordinate plane is the amplitude of a graph.)

A. 2

B. 5

C. 4

D. 2.5

E. 0.3

STOP

This is the End of this Test. You may check your work on this Test if you still have time.

Answer Keys

ACT Math Practice Tests

❋ Now, it's time to review your results to see where you went wrong and what areas you need to improve!

Practice Test 1					
1	A	21	C	41	C
2	D	22	D	42	C
3	B	23	D	43	B
4	E	24	C	44	B
5	C	25	D	45	A
6	C	26	A	46	C
7	A	27	D	47	B
8	C	28	B	48	C
9	E	29	B	49	A
10	D	30	A	50	E
11	B	31	B	51	C
12	B	32	D	52	D
13	A	33	B	53	C
14	D	34	D	54	B
15	A	35	B	55	E
16	C	36	A	56	D
17	B	37	D	57	B
18	B	38	C	58	E
19	D	39	B	59	C
20	E	40	B	60	B

Practice Test 2					
1	D	21	A	41	E
2	A	22	D	42	C
3	A	23	E	43	A
4	B	24	D	44	C
5	D	25	B	45	D
6	E	26	C	46	C
7	B	27	D	47	D
8	E	28	E	48	C
9	C	29	A	49	B
10	B	30	D	50	B
11	A	31	C	51	E
12	A	32	A	52	D
13	B	33	B	53	C
14	E	34	D	54	B
15	E	35	C	55	A
16	B	36	B	56	B
17	C	37	B	57	E
18	C	38	A	58	C
19	E	39	A	59	E
20	A	40	E	60	B

Practice Test 3

1	C	21	C	41	C
2	D	22	D	42	C
3	B	23	D	43	B
4	E	24	C	44	B
5	C	25	D	45	A
6	C	26	A	46	C
7	A	27	D	47	B
8	C	28	B	48	C
9	E	29	B	49	A
10	D	30	A	50	E
11	B	31	B	51	C
12	B	32	D	52	D
13	A	33	B	53	C
14	D	34	D	54	B
15	A	35	B	55	E
16	C	36	A	56	D
17	B	37	D	57	B
18	B	38	C	58	E
19	D	39	B	59	C
20	E	40	B	60	B

Practice Test 4

1	D	21	A	41	E
2	A	22	D	42	C
3	A	23	E	43	A
4	B	24	D	44	C
5	D	25	B	45	D
6	E	26	C	46	C
7	B	27	D	47	D
8	E	28	E	48	C
9	C	29	A	49	B
10	B	30	D	50	B
11	A	31	C	51	E
12	A	32	A	52	D
13	B	33	B	53	C
14	E	34	D	54	B
15	E	35	C	55	A
16	B	36	B	56	B
17	C	37	B	57	E
18	C	38	A	58	C
19	E	39	A	59	E
20	A	40	E	60	B

ACT Practice Tests

Practice Test 5

#		#		#	
1	C	21	C	41	C
2	D	22	D	42	D
3	B	23	D	43	B
4	E	24	C	44	B
5	C	25	D	45	A
6	C	26	A	46	C
7	A	27	D	47	B
8	C	28	B	48	C
9	E	29	B	49	A
10	D	30	A	50	E
11	B	31	B	51	C
12	B	32	D	52	D
13	A	33	B	53	C
14	D	34	D	54	B
15	A	35	B	55	E
16	C	36	A	56	D
17	B	37	D	57	B
18	B	38	C	58	E
19	D	39	B	59	C
20	E	40	B	60	B

Practice Test 6

#		#		#	
1	D	21	A	41	E
2	A	22	D	42	C
3	A	23	E	43	A
4	B	24	D	44	C
5	D	25	B	45	D
6	E	26	C	46	C
7	B	27	D	47	D
8	E	28	E	48	C
9	C	29	A	49	B
10	B	30	D	50	B
11	A	31	C	51	E
12	A	32	A	52	D
13	B	33	B	53	C
14	E	34	D	54	B
15	E	35	C	55	A
16	B	36	B	56	B
17	C	37	B	57	E
18	C	38	A	58	C
19	E	39	A	59	E
20	A	40	E	60	B

Answers and Explanations

Answers and Explanations

ACT Mathematics

Practice Tests 1

1) Answer: A.

$$7^{\frac{5}{3}} \times 7^{\frac{1}{3}} = 7^{\frac{5}{3}+\frac{1}{3}} = 7^{\frac{6}{3}} = 7^2$$

2) Answer: D.

Solve for x, $\frac{4x}{25} = \frac{x-1}{5}$

Multiply the second fraction by 5, $\frac{4x}{25} = \frac{5(x-1)}{5\times5}$

Tow denominators are equal. Therefore, the numerators must be equal.

$4x = 5x - 5 \rightarrow -x = -5 \rightarrow x = 5$

3) Answer: B.

Simplify each option provided.

A. $20 - (4 \times 10) + (6 \times 30) = 20 - 40 + 180 = 160$

B. $\left(\frac{11}{8} \times 72\right) + \left(\frac{125}{5}\right) = 99 + 25 = 124$(this is the answer)

C. $\left(\left(\frac{30}{4} + \frac{13}{2}\right) \times 7\right) - \frac{11}{2} + \frac{110}{4} = \left(\left(\frac{30+26}{4}\right) \times 7\right) - \frac{11}{2} + \frac{55}{2} = \left(\left(\frac{56}{4}\right) \times 7\right) + \frac{55-11}{2} =$

   $(14 \times 7) + \frac{44}{2} = 98 + 22 = 120$

D. $(2 \times 10) + (50 \times 1.5) + 15 = 20 + 75 + 15 = 110$

E. $\frac{481}{6} + \frac{121}{3} = \frac{481+242}{6} = 120.5$

4) Answer: E.

six years ago, Amy was two times as old as Mike. Mike is 14 years

now. Therefore, 6 years ago Mike was 8 years.

Six years ago, Amy was: $A = 2 \times 8 = 16$

Now Amy is 22 years old: $16 + 6 = 22$

5) Answer: C.

Set of number that are not composite between 1 and 15: A= {1,2, 3, 5, 7, 11, 13}

$$\text{Probability} = \frac{number\ of\ desired\ outcomes}{number\ of\ total\ outcomes} = \frac{7}{15}$$

6) Answer: C.

I. $|a| < 2 \to -2 < a < 2$

Multiply all sides by b. Since, $b > 0 \to -2b < ba < 2b$ (it is true!)

II. Since, $-2 < a < 2, and\ a < 0 \to -a > a^2 > a$ (plug in $-\frac{1}{2}$, and check!) (It's false)

III. $-2 < a < 2, multiply\ all\ sides\ by\ 2, then: -4 < 2a < 4$

Subtract 3 from all sides. Then:

$-4 - 3 < 2a - 3 < 2 - 3 \to -7 < 2a - 3 < 1$ (It is true!)

7) Answer: A.

Check each option provided:

A. 1 $\quad \frac{4+5+8+11+12}{5} = \frac{40}{5} = 8$

B. 4 $\quad \frac{1+5+8+11+12}{5} = \frac{37}{5} = 7.4$

C. 5 $\quad \frac{1+4+8+11+12}{5} = \frac{36}{5} = 7.2$

D. 11 $\quad \frac{1+4+5+8+12}{5} = \frac{30}{5} = 6$

E. 12 $\quad \frac{1+4+5+8+11}{5} = \frac{29}{5} = 5.8$

8) Answer: C.

The weight of 12.2 meters of this rope is: $13.2 \times 700\ g = 9,240\ g$

$1\ kg = 1,000\ g$, therefore, $9,240\ g \div 1,000 = 9.24\ kg$

9) Answer: E.

$y = 5ab + 2b^3$, Plug in the values of a and b in the equation: $a = 3$ and $b = 1$

$y = 5\ (3)\ (1) + 2\ (1)^3 = 15 + 2(1) = 15 + 2 = 17$

10) Answer: D.

$(g-f)(x) = g(x) - f(x) = (-x^2 - 2 - 3x) - (6 + x)$

$-x^2 - 2 - 3x - 6 - x = -x^2 - 4x - 8$

11) Answer: B.

To find the discount, multiply the number by (100% – rate of discount).

Therefore, for the first discount we get: (D) (100% – 40%) = (D) (0.60) = 0.60 D

For increase of 10 %: (0.60 D) (100% + 10%) = (0.60 D) (1.10) = 0.66 D = 66% of D

12) Answer: B.

1,000 times the number is 60.5. Let x be the number, then:

$1,000x = 60.5 \rightarrow x = \frac{60.5}{1,000} = 0.0605$

13) Answer: A.

Let's review the options provided.

A. 4. In 4 years, David will be 48 and Ava will be 12. 48 is 4 times 12.

B. 6. In 6 years, David will be 50 and Ava will be 14. 50 is NOT 4 times 14!

C. 8. In 8 years, David will be 52 and Ava will be 16. 52 is not 4 times 16.

D. 10. In 10 years, David will be 54 and Ava will be 18. 54 is not 4 times 18.

E. 14. In 14 years, David will be 58 and Ava will be 22. 58 is not 4 times 20.

14) Answer: D.

The area of the floor is: 7 cm × 32cm = 224cm

The number is tiles needed = 224 ÷ 8 = 28

15) Answer: A.

Write the numbers in order: 3, 6, 7, 8, 15, 17, 21

Since we have 7 numbers (7 is odd), then the median is the number in the middle,

which is 8.

16) Answer: C.

Employer's revenue: $0.3x + 8000$

17) Answer: B.

The diagonal of the square is 6. Let x be the side.

Use Pythagorean Theorem: $a^2 + b^2 = c^2$

$x^2 + x^2 = 6^2 \Rightarrow 2x^2 = 6^2 \Rightarrow 2x^2 = 36 \Rightarrow x^2 = 18 \Rightarrow x = \sqrt{18}$

The area of the square is: $\sqrt{18} \times \sqrt{18} = 18$

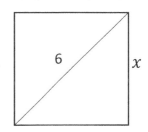

18) Answer: B.

$x = 30 + 135 = 165$

19) Answer: D.

By definition, the sine of any acute angle is equal to the cosine of its complement.

Since, angle A and B are complementary angles, therefore:

$sin\ A\ =\ cos\ B$

20) Answer: E.

Solve the system of equations by elimination method.

$4x - 2y = -20$
$\underline{-x + y = 10}$ Multiply the second equation by 4, then add it to the first equation.

$\begin{matrix} 4x - 2y = -20 \\ 4(-x + y = 10) \end{matrix} \Rightarrow \begin{matrix} 4x - 2y = -20 \\ -4x + 4y = 40) \end{matrix} \Rightarrow$ add the equations

$2y = 20 \Rightarrow y = 10$

21) Answer: C.

Use distance formula:

Distance = Rate × time $\Rightarrow$ 430 = 50 × T, divide both sides by 50.

430 / 50 = T $\Rightarrow$ T = 8.6hours.

Change hours to minutes for the decimal part. 0.6 hours = 0.6 × 60 = 36 minutes.

22) Answer: D.

x and z are colinear. y and $4x$ are colinear. Therefore,

$x + z = y + 4x, subtract\ x\ from\ both\ sides, then, z = y + 3x$

23) Answer: D.

Check each option.

A. $\frac{1}{4} > 0.15$ $\frac{1}{4} = 0.25$ and it is less than 0.15. Not true!

B. $10\% = \frac{3}{5}$ $10\% = \frac{1}{10} < \frac{3}{5}$. Not True!

C. $3 < \frac{3}{2}$ $\frac{3}{2} = 1.5 < 3$. Not True!

D. $\frac{4}{6} > 0.6$ $\frac{4}{6} = 0.6666 ...$ and it is greater than 0.6. Bingo!

E. None of them above   Not True!

24) Answer: C.

30% of 80 equals to: $0.30 \times 80 = 24$

18% of 800 equals to: $0.18 \times 800 = 144$

30% of 80 is added to 18% of 800: $24 + 144 = 168$

25) Answer: D.

The relationship among all sides of special right triangle

$30° - 60° - 90°$ is provided in this triangle:

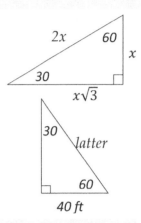

In this triangle, the opposite side of $30°$ angle is half of the

hypotenuse. Draw the shape of this question.

The latter is the hypotenuse.

Therefore, the latter is 80 ft.

26) Answer: A.

The percent of girls playing tennis is: $60\% \times 15\% = 0.60 \times 0.15 = 0.090 = 9\%$

27) Answer: D.

Solve for x. $x^3 + 18 = 140 \Rightarrow x^3 = 122$

Let's review the options.

   A. 1 and 2. $1^3 = 1$ and $2^3 = 8$, 122 is not between these two numbers.

   B. 2 and 3. $2^3 = 8$ and $3^3 = 27$, 122 is not between these two numbers.

   C. 3 and 4. $3^3 = 27$ and $4^3 = 64$, 122 is not between these two numbers.

   D. 4 and 5. $4^3 = 64$ and $5^3 = 125$, 122 is between these two numbers.

   E. 5 and 6. $5^3 = 125$ and $6^3 = 216$, 122 is not between these two numbers.

28) Answer: B.

$(x - 2)^3 = 8 \rightarrow x - 2 = 2 \rightarrow x = 4$

$\rightarrow (x - 3)(x - 2) = (4 - 3)(4 - 2) = (1)(2) = 2$

29) Answer: B.

$3x^2 + 4y^5 - x^2 + 3z^3 - 2y^2 + 3x^3 - 3y^5 + 4z^3 = 3x^2 - x^2 + 3x^3 - 2y^2 + 4y^5 -$

$3y^5 + 3z^3 + 4z^3 = 2x^2 + 3x^3 - 2y^2 + y^5 + 7z^3$

30) Answer: A.

Add the first 5 numbers. $40 + 42 + 55 + 38 + 50 = 225$

To find the distance traveled in the next 5 hours, multiply the average by number of hours.

Distance = Average × Rate = $60 × 5 = 300$

Add both numbers. $300 + 225 = 525$

31) Answer: B.

The question is this: 1.38 is what percent of 1.15?

Use percent formula: part $= \frac{\text{percent}}{100} \times$ whole

$1.38 = \frac{\text{percent}}{100} \times 1.15 \Rightarrow 1.38 = \frac{\text{percent} \times 1.15}{100} \Rightarrow 138 = \text{percent} \times 1.15$

$\Rightarrow \text{percent} = \frac{138}{1.15} = 120$

32) Answer: D.

We know that: $i = \sqrt{-1} \Rightarrow i^2 = -1$

$(-4 + 8i)(3 + 5i) = -12 - 20i + 24i + 40i^2 = -12 + 4i - 40 = 4i - 52$

33) Answer: B.

$tan\theta = \frac{\text{opposite}}{\text{adjacent}}$

$tan\theta = \frac{3}{4} \Rightarrow$ we have the following right triangle. Then,

$c = \sqrt{3^2 + 4^2} = \sqrt{9 + 16} = \sqrt{25} = 5$

$cos\theta = \frac{adjacent}{hypotenuse} = \frac{4}{5}$

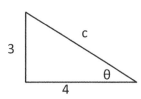

34) Answer: D.

The amplitude in the graph of the equation $y = acosbx$ is a. (a and b are constant)

In the equation $y = cosx$, the amplitude is 2 and the period of the graph is 2π.

The only option that has two times the amplitude of graph $y = cos\ x$ is $y = 2 + 2cos\ x$

They both have the amplitude of 2 and period of 2π.

35) Answer: B.

$\frac{1}{3} \cong 0.33$ $\frac{4}{7} \cong 0.57$ $\frac{7}{11} \cong 0.63$ $\frac{3}{4} = 0.75$

36) Answer: A.

Let x be the number of years. Therefore, $2,000 per year equals $2000x$.

starting from $22,000 annual salary means you should add that amount to $2000x$.

Income more than that is: $I > 2,000\,x + 22,000$.

37) Answer: D.

Percentage of men in city C $= \frac{700}{1365} \times 100 = 51.28\%$

Percentage of men in city B $= \frac{300}{591} \times 100 = 50.76\%$

Percentage of men in city C to percentage of men in city B: $\frac{51.28}{50.76} = 1.01$

38) Answer: C.

Ratio of women to men in city A: $\frac{570}{600} = 0.95$

Ratio of women to men in city B: $\frac{291}{300} = 0.97$

Ratio of women to men in city C: $\frac{665}{700} = 0.95$

Ratio of women to men in city D: $\frac{528}{550} = 0.96$

39) Answer: B.

Let the number of women should be added to city D be x, then:

$\frac{528 + x}{550} = 1.3 \rightarrow 528 + x = 550 \times 1.3 = 715 \rightarrow x = 187$

40) Answer: B.

We write the numbers in the order: 1, 1, 2, 2, 3, 3, 3, 4, 4, 4, 5

The mode of numbers is: 3 and 4, median is: 3

41) Answer: C.

Let the number be A. Then: $x = y\% \times A \rightarrow$ (Solve for A)$\rightarrow x = \frac{y}{100} \times A$

Multiply both sides by $\frac{100}{y}$: $x \times \frac{100}{y} = \frac{y}{100} \times \frac{100}{y} \times A \rightarrow A = \frac{100x}{y}$

42) Answer: C.

$$tangent \ \beta = \frac{1}{cotangent \ \beta} = \frac{1}{1} = 1$$

43) Answer: B.

$$\frac{3}{4} \times 80 = 60$$

44) Answer: B.

One liter=1,000 cm^3 → 4 liters=4,000 cm^3

$4,000 = 20 \times 5 \times h \rightarrow h = \frac{4,000}{100} = 40$ cm

45) Answer: A.

Surface Area of a cylinder = $2\pi r \ (r \ + \ h)$,

The radius of the cylinder is 2 (4÷2) inches and its height is 7 inches. Therefore,

Surface Area of a cylinder = $2\pi \ (2) \ (2 + 7) = 36 \ \pi$

46) Answer: C.

3% of the volume of the solution is alcohol. Let x be the volume of the solution.

Then: 3% of x = 21ml ⇒ $0.03 \ x = 21 \Rightarrow x = 21 \div 0.03 = 700$

47) Answer: B.

$|x - 8| \leq 2 \rightarrow -2 \leq x - 8 \leq 2 \rightarrow -2 + 8 \leq x - 8 + 8 \leq 2 + 8 \rightarrow 6 \leq x \leq 10$

48) Answer: C.

Plug in each pair of number in the equation:

A. $(3, -1)$: $4 \ (3) - (-1) = 13$ Nope!

B. $(-1, 3)$: $4 \ (-1) - (3) = -7$ Nope!

C. $(-1, -1)$: $4 \ (-1) - (-1) = -3$ Bingo!

D. $(3, -3)$: $4 \ (3) - (-3) = 15$ Nope!

E. $(0, -3)$: $4 \ (0) - (-3) = 3$ Nope!

49) Answer: A.

The area of ΔBED is 10, then: $\frac{5 \times AB}{2} = 10 \rightarrow 5 \times AB = 20 \rightarrow AB = 4$

The area of ΔBDF is 12, then: $\frac{4 \times BC}{2} = 12 \rightarrow 4 \times BC = 24 \rightarrow BC = 6$

The perimeter of the rectangle is = $2 \times (4 + 6) = 20$

50) Answer: E.

The slop of line A is: $m = \frac{y_2 - y_1}{x_2 - x_1} = \frac{6-5}{5-4} = 1$

Parallel lines have the same slope and only choice E $(y = x)$ has slope of 1.

51) Answer: C.

When points are reflected over y-axis, the value of y in the coordinates doesn't change and the sign of x changes. Therefore, the coordinates of point B is $(-6, 2)$.

52) Answer: D.

If 15 balls are removed from the bag at random, there will be one ball in the bag. The probability of choosing a brown ball is 1 out of 16. Therefore, the probability of not choosing a brown ball is 15 out of 16 and the probability of having not a brown ball after removing 15 balls is the same.

53) Answer: C.

Write a proportion and solve for x.

$\frac{5}{3} = \frac{x}{48} \Rightarrow 3x = 5 \times 48 \Rightarrow x = 80$ ft

54) Answer: B.

The area of trapezoid is: $\left(\frac{9+15}{2}\right) \times x = 96 \rightarrow 12x = 96 \rightarrow x = 8$

$y = \sqrt{8^2 + 6^2} = 10$

Perimeter is: $15 + 8 + 9 + 10 = 42$

55) Answer: E.

$0.6x = (0.2) \times 30 \rightarrow x = 10 \rightarrow (x + 2)^2 = (12)^2 = 144$

56) Answer: D.

$g(x) = -1$, then $f(g(x)) = f(-1) = 2(-1)^3 + 5(-1)^2 + 2(-1) = -2 + 5 - 2 = 1$

57) Answer: B.

Use the information provided in the question to draw the shape.

Use Pythagorean Theorem: $a^2 + b^2 = c^2$

$50^2 + 120^2 = c^2 \Rightarrow 2,500 + 1,400 = c^2$

$\Rightarrow 16,900 = c^2 \Rightarrow c = 130$

58) Answer: E.

$$\begin{cases} 2x = x + 3y - 5 \\ 6x = 8y + 10 \end{cases} \rightarrow \begin{cases} x - 3y = -5 \\ 6x - 8y = 10 \end{cases}$$

Multiply first equation by -6.

$$\begin{cases} -6x + 18y = 30 \\ 6x - 8y = 10 \end{cases} \rightarrow \text{add two equations.}$$

$10y = 40 \rightarrow y = 4 \rightarrow x = 7 \rightarrow x \times y = 28$

59) Answer: C.

To solve for $f(2g(p))$, first, find $2g(p)$

$g(x) = log_2 x \rightarrow g(p) = log_2 p \rightarrow 2g(p) = 2log_2 p = log_2 p^2$

Now, find $f(2g(p))$: $f(x) = 2^x \rightarrow f(log_2 p^2) = 2^{log_2 p^2}$

Logarithms and exponentials with the same base cancel each other. This is true because logarithms and exponentials are inverse operations. Then: $f(log_2 p^2) = 2^{log_2 p^2} = p^2$

60) Answer: B.

$$x_1 = \frac{8y + \frac{r}{r+1}}{\frac{10}{\frac{z}{5}}} = \frac{8y + \frac{r}{r+1}}{\frac{5 \times 10}{z}} = \frac{8y + \frac{r}{r+1}}{5 \times \frac{10}{z}} = \frac{1}{5} \times \frac{8y + \frac{r}{r+1}}{10} = \frac{x}{5}$$

Answers and Explanations

ACT Mathematics

Practice Tests 2

1) Answer: D.

$840,000 = 8.4 \times 10^5$

2) Answer: A.

$(x^6)^{\frac{5}{8}} = x^{6 \times \frac{5}{8}} = x^{\frac{30}{8}} = x^{\frac{15}{4}}$

3) Answer: A.

To simplify the fraction, multiply both numerator and denominator by i. $\frac{2-5i}{-2i} \times \frac{i}{i} =$

$\frac{2i-2i^2}{-2i^2}$

$i^2 - 1$, Then: $\frac{2i-5i^2}{-2i^2} = \frac{2i-5(-1)}{-2(-1)} = \frac{2i+5}{2} = \frac{2i}{2} + \frac{5}{2} = i + \frac{5}{2}$

4) Answer: B.

$625 = 5^4 \quad \rightarrow 5^x = 5^4 \rightarrow x = 4$

5) Answer: D.

Here is the list of all prime numbers between 10 and 20:

11, 13, 17, 19

The sum of all prime numbers between 10 and 20 is:

$11 + 13 + 17 + 19 = 60$

6) Answer: E.

Solve for x. $\sqrt{7x} = \sqrt{y}$; Square both sides of the equation: $(\sqrt{7x})^2 = (\sqrt{y})^2$

$7x = y \rightarrow x = \frac{y}{7}$

7) Answer: B.

$\text{average} = \frac{\text{sum of terms}}{\text{number of terms}}$

The sum of the weight of all girls is: $20 \times 60 = 1,200 \text{ kg}$

The sum of the weight of all boys is: $30 \times 65 = 1,950 \text{ kg}$

The sum of the weight of all students is: $1,080 + 1,984 = 3,150$ kg

$$\text{average} = \frac{3,150}{50} = 63$$

8) Answer: E.

$$y = (-2x^3)^2 = (-2)^2(x^3)^2 = 4x^6$$

9) Answer: C.

Plug in the value of x and y.

$x = 3$ and $y = -4$

$3(x - y) + (1 - x)^2 = 3(3 - (-4)) + (1 - 3)^2 = 3(3 + 4) + (-2)^2 = 21 + 4 = 25$

10) Answer: B.

The question is this: 399.75 is what percent of 615?

Use percent formula: $\text{part} = \frac{\text{percent}}{100} \times \text{whole}$

$399.75 = \frac{\text{percent}}{100} \times 615 \Rightarrow 399.75 = \frac{\text{percent} \times 615}{100} \Rightarrow 39,975 = \text{percent} \times 615 \Rightarrow$

$\text{percent} = \frac{39,975}{615} = 65$

399.75 is 65 % of 615. Therefore, the discount is: $100\% - 65\% = 35\%$

11) Answer: A.

$$\left(\frac{f}{g}\right)(x) = \frac{f(x)}{g(x)} = \frac{2x - 1}{x^2 - 2x}$$

12) Answer: A.

The equation of a line is: $y = mx + b$, where m is the slope and b is the y-intercept.

First find the slope: $m = \frac{y_2 - y_1}{x_2 - x_1} = \frac{10 - (-5)}{8 - 3} = \frac{15}{5} = 3$

Then, we have: $y = 3x + b$

Choose one point and plug in the values of x and y in the equation to solve for b.

Let's choose the point $(3, -5)$

$y = 3x + b \rightarrow -5 = 3(3) + b \rightarrow -5 = 9 + b \rightarrow b = -14$

The equation of the line is: $y = 3x - 14$

13) Answer: B.

Use simple interest formula:

$I = prt$ (I = interest, p = principal, r = rate, t = time)

$I = (15,000)(0.025)(2) = 750$

14) Answer: E.

Number of visiting fans: $\frac{3 \times 25,000}{5} = 15,000$

15) Answer: E.

The sum of all angles in a quadrilateral is 360 degrees.

Let x be the smallest angle in the quadrilateral. Then the angles are: $x, 2x, 2x, 5x$

$x + 2x + 4x + 5x = 360 \rightarrow 12x = 360 \rightarrow x = 30$

The angles in the quadrilateral are: $30°, 60°, 120°,$ and $150°$

16) Answer: B.

$sin^2 a + cos^2 a = 1$, then:

$x + 1 = 3 \rightarrow x = 2$

17) Answer: C.

Formula for the area of a circle is: $A = \pi r^2$

Using 81 for the area of the circle we have: $81 = \pi r^2$

Let's solve for the radius (r).

$\frac{81}{\pi} = r^2 \rightarrow r = \sqrt{\frac{81}{\pi}} = \frac{9}{\sqrt{\pi}} = \frac{9}{\sqrt{\pi}} \times \frac{\sqrt{\pi}}{\sqrt{\pi}} = \frac{9\sqrt{\pi}}{\pi}$

18) Answer: C.

Length of the rectangle is: $\frac{3}{4} \times 24 = 18$

perimeter of rectangle is: $2 \times (18 + 24) = 84$

19) Answer: E.

The angle x and 55 are complementary angles. Therefore:

$x + 55 = 180$

$180° - 55° = 125°$

20) Answer: A.

Solving Systems of Equations by Elimination

Multiply the first equation by (–3), then add it to the second equation.

$$\begin{array}{l} -3(2x + 3y = \ 10) \\ \underline{6x - 3y = -18} \end{array} \Rightarrow \begin{array}{l} -6x - 9y = -30 \\ \underline{6x - 3y = -18} \end{array} \Rightarrow -12y = -48 \Rightarrow y = 4$$

Plug in the value of y into one of the equations and solve for x.

$$2x + 3(4) = \ 10 \Rightarrow 2x + 12 = \ 10 \Rightarrow 2x = -2 \Rightarrow x = -1$$

21) Answer: A.

The sum of supplement angles is 180. Let x be that angle. Therefore, $x + 8x = 180 \Rightarrow 9x = 180$, divide both sides by 9: $x = 20$

22) Answer: D.

Three times of 28,000 is 84,000. One sixth of them cancelled their tickets.

One sixth of 84,000 equal 14,000 ($1/6 \times 84,000 = 14,000$).

70,000 ($84,000 - 14,000 = 70,000$) fans are attending this week

23) Answer: E.

$sin a = \frac{1}{2} \Rightarrow$ Since $sin a = \frac{opposite}{hypotenuse}$, we have the following right triangle. Then,

$c = \sqrt{4^2 - 2^2} = \sqrt{16 - 4} = \sqrt{12}$

$cos a = \frac{\sqrt{12}}{4} = \frac{\sqrt{4} \times \sqrt{3}}{4} = \frac{\sqrt{3}}{2}$

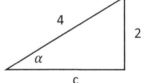

24) Answer: D.

In any rectangle measure of all angles equals 360°.

25) Answer: B.

The equation of a circle in standard form is:

$(x - h)^2 + (y - k)^2 = r^2$, where r is the radius of the circle.

In this circle the radius is 3. $r^2 = 9 \rightarrow r = 3$

$(x + 2)^2 + (y - 4)^2 = 9$

Area of a circle: $A = \pi r^2 = \pi(3)^2 = 9\pi$

26) Answer: C.

the population is increased by 15% and 20%. 15% increase changes the population to 115% of original population.

For the second increase, multiply the result by 120%.

$(1.15) \times (1.20) = 1.38 = 138\%$

38 percent of the population is increased after two years.

27) Answer: D.

$4x^2y^3 + 5x^3y^5 - (5x^2y^3 - 2x^3y^5) = 4x^2y^3 - 5x^2y^3 + 5x^3y^5 + 2x^3y^5 = 7x^3y^5 - x^2y^3$

28) Answer: E.

Frist factor the function: $f(x) = x^3 + 5x^2 + 6x = x(x+2)(x+3)$

To find the zeros, $f(x)$ should be zero. $f(x) = x(x+2)(x+3) = 0$

Therefore, the zeros are: $x = 0$

$(x+2) = 0 \Rightarrow x = -2 \, ; (x+3) = 0 \Rightarrow x = -3$

29) Answer: A.

The relationship among all sides of right triangle $30° - 60° - 90°$ is provided in the

following triangle:

Sine of $30°$ equals to: $\dfrac{opposite}{hypotenuse} = \dfrac{x}{2x} = \dfrac{1}{2}$

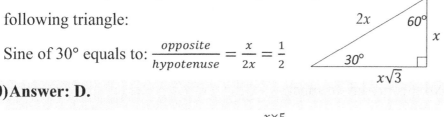

30) Answer: D.

Let x be the length of AB, then: $15 = \dfrac{x \times 5}{2} \rightarrow x = 6$

The length of AC $= \sqrt{6^2 + 8^2} = \sqrt{100} = 10$

The perimeter of $\Delta ABC = 6 + 8 + 10 = 24$

31) Answer: C.

$x_{1,2} = \dfrac{-b \pm \sqrt{b^2 - 4ac}}{2a}$

$ax^2 + bx + c = 0 \Rightarrow x^2 + 2x - 5 = 0$, then: a = 1, b = 2 and c = -5

$x = \dfrac{-2 + \sqrt{2^2 - 4.1.-5}}{2.1} = \sqrt{6} - 1 \, ; \; x = \dfrac{-2 - \sqrt{2^2 - 4.1.-5}}{2.1} = -1 - \sqrt{6}$

32) Answer: A.

Let x be the cost of one-kilogram orange, then:

$3x + (2 \times 3.6) = 34.2 \rightarrow 3x + 7.2 = 34.2 \rightarrow 3x = 34.2 - 7.2 \rightarrow 3x = 27$

$\rightarrow x = \dfrac{27}{3} = \$9$

33) Answer: B.

Simplify the expression.

$$\sqrt{\frac{x^2}{3} + \frac{x^2}{9}} = \sqrt{\frac{3x^2}{9} + \frac{x^2}{9}} = \sqrt{\frac{4x^2}{9}} = \sqrt{\frac{4}{9}x^2} = \sqrt{\frac{4}{9}} \times \sqrt{x^2} = \frac{2}{3} \times x = \frac{2x}{3}$$

34) Answer: D.

First find the number of pants sold in each month.

January: 110, February: 88, March: 90, April: 70, May: 84, June: 65

Check each option provided.

A. There is a decrease from January to February

B. February and March, $\left(\frac{90-88}{90}\right) \times 100 = \frac{2}{90} \times 100 = 2.22\%$

C. There is a decrease from March to April

D. April and May: there is an increase from April to May

$\left(\frac{84-70}{70}\right) \times 100 = \frac{14}{70} \times 100 = 20\%$

E. There is a decrease from May to June.

35) Answer: C.

First, order the number of shirts sold each month:

$130, 140, 144, 150, 160, 170$

mean is: $\frac{130+140+144+150+160+170}{6} = \frac{894}{6} = 149$

Put the number of shoes sold per month in order:

$20, 25, 25, 35, 35, 40$; median is: $\frac{25+35}{2} = 30$

36) Answer: B.

The ratio of number of pants to number of shoes in May equals $\frac{84}{25}$.

Five-seventeenth of this ratio is $\left(\frac{5}{12}\right)\left(\frac{84}{25}\right)$. Now, let x be the number of shoes needed to be added in April.

$\frac{70}{20+x} = \left(\frac{5}{12}\right)\left(\frac{84}{25}\right) \rightarrow \frac{70}{20+x} = \frac{420}{300} = 1.4 \rightarrow 70 = 1.4(20+x) \rightarrow 70 = 28 + 1.4x \rightarrow$

$1.4x = 42 \rightarrow x = 30$

37) Answer: B.

The probability of choosing a diamond is 13/52 = ¼

38) Answer: A.

Let x be the number of shoes the team can purchase. Therefore, the team can purchase $10\,x$.

The team had \$30,000 and spent \$24,000. Now the team can spend on new shoes \$6,000 at most.

Now, write the inequality: $140x + 24{,}000 \leq 30{,}000$

39) Answer: A.

Plug in the value of x in the equation and solve for y.

$3y = \frac{2x^2}{3} + 6 \to 3y = \frac{2(9)^2}{3} + 6 \to 3y = \frac{2(81)}{3} + 6 \to 3y = 54 + 6 = 60 \to 3y = 60 \to y = 20$

40) Answer: E.

Use formula of rectangle prism volume.

V = (length) (width) (height) $\Rightarrow 3{,}000 =$ (15) (10) (height) $\Rightarrow$ height = $3{,}000 \div 150 = 20$

41) Answer: E.

Th ratio of boy to girls is 2:6. Therefore, there are 2 boys out of 8 students. To find the answer, first divide the total number of students by 8, then multiply the result by 2.

$800 \div 8 = 100 \Rightarrow 100 \times 2 = 200$

42) Answer: C.

Plug in the value of each option in the inequality.

A. $2(2 - 3)^2 + 1 > 3(2) - 1 \to 2 > 5$ No!

B. $6(6 - 3)^2 + 1 > 3(6) - 1 \to 10 > 17$ No!

C. $8(8 - 3)^2 + 1 > 3(8) - 1 \to 26 > 23$ Bingo!

D. $3(3 - 3)^2 + 1 > 3(3) - 1 \to 1 > 8$ No!

E. $4(4 - 3)^2 + 1 > 3(4) - 1 \to 2 > 11$ No!

43) Answer: A.

$(x + 3)(x + p) = x^2 + (3 + p)x + 3p \to 3 + p = 4 \to p = 1 \; and \; r = 3p = 3$

44) Answer: C.

First, find the number.

Let x be the number. Write the equation and solve for x.

120 % of a number is 72, then:

$1.2 \times x = 72 \Rightarrow x = 72 \div 1.2 = 60$

80 % of 60 is: $0.8 \times 60 = 48$

45) Answer: D.

If the length of the box is 36, then the width of the box is one third of it, 12, and the height of the box is 4 (one third of the width). The volume of the box is:

V = (length) × (width) × (height) = (36) × (12) × (4) = 1,728

46) Answer: C.

Let x be the smallest number. Then, these are the numbers:

$x, x + 1, x + 2, x + 3, x + 4$

average $= \dfrac{\text{sum of terms}}{\text{number of terms}} \Rightarrow 36 = \dfrac{x+(x+1)+(x+2)+(x+3)+(x+4)}{5} \Rightarrow 36 = \dfrac{5x+10}{5} \Rightarrow 180 =$

$5x + 10 \Rightarrow 170 = 5x \Rightarrow x = 34$

47) Answer: D.

Formula for the Surface area of a cylinder is:

$SA = 2\pi r^2 + 2\pi rh \rightarrow 120\pi = 2\pi r^2 + 2\pi r(7) \rightarrow r^2 + 7r - 60 = 0$

Factorize and solve for r.

$(r + 12)(r - 5) = 0 \rightarrow r = 5 \quad or \quad r = -12 \ (unacceptable)$

48) Answer: C.

Since the triangle ABC is reflected over the y-axis, then all values of y's of the points don't change and the sign of all x's change.

(remember that when a point is reflected over the y-axis, the value of y does not change and when a point is reflected over the x-axis, the value of x does not change).

Therefore:

$(4, -2)$ changes to $(-4, -2)$

$(-2, -3)$ changes to $(2, -3)$

$(3,5)$ changes to $(-3,5)$

49) Answer: B.

The equation of a line in slope intercept form is: $y = mx + b$

Solve for y.

$8x - 4y = 16 \Rightarrow -4y = 16 - 8x \Rightarrow y = (16 - 8x) \div (-4) \Rightarrow$

$y = 2x - 4 \rightarrow$ The slope is 2.

The slope of the line perpendicular to this line is:

$m_1 \times m_2 = -1 \Rightarrow 2 \times m_2 = -1 \Rightarrow m_2 = -\frac{1}{2}$

50) Answer: B.

The area of rectangle is: $8 \times 5 = 40 \text{ cm}^2$

The area of circle is: $\pi r^2 = \pi \times (\frac{12}{2})^2 = 3 \times 36 = 108 \ cm^2$

Difference of areas is: $108 - 40 = 68$

51) Answer: E.

$f\big(g(x)\big) = 3 \times (\frac{1}{x})^3 + 3 = \frac{3}{x^3} + 3$

52) Answer: D.

Use the information provided in the question to draw
the shape. Use Pythagorean Theorem: $a^2 + b^2 = c^2$

$50^2 + 120^2 = c^2 \Rightarrow 2,500 + 14,400 = c^2$

$\Rightarrow 16,900 = c^2 \Rightarrow c = 130$

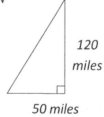

53) Answer: C.

Let L be the length of the rectangular and W be the with of the rectangular. Then, $L = 3W + 2$

The perimeter of the rectangle is 36 meters. Therefore:

$$2L + 2W = 36$$

$$L + W = 18$$

Replace the value of L from the first equation into the second equation and solve for W:

$$(3W + 2) + W = 18 \rightarrow 4W + 2 = 18 \rightarrow 4W = 16 \rightarrow W = 4$$

The width of the rectangle is 4 meters and its length is: $L = 3W + 2 = 3(4) + 2 = 14$

The area of the rectangle is: length × width = $14 \times 4 = 56$

54) Answer: B.

Let x be the number of adult tickets and y be the number of student tickets. Then:

$x + y = 16$

$12.50x + 6.50y = 128$

Use elimination method to solve this system of equation. Multiply the first equation by -6.5 and add it to the second equation.

$-6.5(x + y = 16) \Rightarrow -6.5x - 6.5y = -104$

$12.50x + 6.50y = 128 \Rightarrow 6x = 24 \rightarrow x = 4$

There are 4 adults' tickets and 12 student tickets.

55) Answer: A.

$x - 2 \geq 4 \rightarrow x \geq 4 + 2 \rightarrow x \geq 6$

Or $x - 2 \leq -4 \rightarrow x \leq -4 + 2 \rightarrow x \leq -2$

Then, solution is: $\quad x \geq 6 \cup x \leq -2$

56) Answer: B.

$\tan = \frac{opposite}{adjacent}$, and $\tan x = \frac{5}{12}$, therefore, the opposite side of the angle x is 5 and the adjacent side is 12. Let's draw the triangle.

Using Pythagorean theorem, we have:

$a^2 + b^2 = c^2 \rightarrow 5^2 + 12^2 = c^2 \rightarrow 25 + 144 = c^2 \rightarrow c = 13$

$\sin x = \frac{opposite}{hypotenuse} = \frac{5}{13}$

57) Answer: E.

Based on triangle similarity theorem:

$\frac{a}{a+b} = \frac{c}{5} \rightarrow c = \frac{5a}{a+b} = \frac{5\sqrt{3}}{\sqrt{3}+4\sqrt{3}} = 1$

$\rightarrow$ area of shaded region is: $\left(\frac{c+5}{2}\right)(b) = 3 \times 4\sqrt{3} = 12\sqrt{3}$

58) Answer: C.

Write the ratio of $7a$ to $3b$, $\frac{7a}{3b} = \frac{1}{15}$

Use cross multiplication and then simplify.

$$7a \times 15 = 3b \times 1 \rightarrow 105a = 3b \rightarrow a = \frac{3b}{105} = \frac{b}{35}$$

Now, find the ratio of a to b.

$$\frac{a}{b} = \frac{\frac{b}{35}}{b} \rightarrow \frac{b}{35} \div b = \frac{b}{35} \times \frac{1}{b} = \frac{b}{35b} = \frac{1}{35}$$

59) Answer: E.

First, find $2A$.

$$A = \begin{bmatrix} -1 & 3 \\ 1 & -3 \end{bmatrix} \Rightarrow 2A = 2 \times \begin{bmatrix} -1 & 3 \\ 1 & -3 \end{bmatrix} = \begin{bmatrix} -2 & 6 \\ 2 & -6 \end{bmatrix}$$

Now, solve for $2A - B$:

$$\begin{bmatrix} -2 & 6 \\ 2 & -6 \end{bmatrix} - \begin{bmatrix} 5 & 1 \\ -3 & 4 \end{bmatrix} = \begin{bmatrix} -2-5 & 6-1 \\ 2-(-3) & -6-4 \end{bmatrix} = \begin{bmatrix} -7 & 5 \\ 5 & -10 \end{bmatrix}$$

60) Answer: B.

The amplitude in the graph of the equation $y = acosbx$ is a. (a and b are constant)

In the equation $y - 1 = 3cos2x$, the amplitude is 3.

Answers and Explanations

ACT Mathematics

Practice Tests 3

1) Answer: C.

$$4^{\frac{7}{3}} \times 4^{\frac{2}{3}} = 4^{\frac{7}{3} + \frac{2}{3}} = 4^{\frac{9}{3}} = 4^3$$

2) Answer: D.

Solve for x, $\frac{4x}{25} = \frac{x-1}{5}$

Multiply the second fraction by 5, $\frac{4x}{25} = \frac{5(x-1)}{5 \times 5}$

Tow denominators are equal. Therefore, the numerators must be equal.

$4x = 5x - 5 \rightarrow -x = -5 \rightarrow x = 5$

3) Answer: B.

Simplify each option provided.

A. $20 - (4 \times 10) + (6 \times 30) = 20 - 40 + 180 = 160$

B. $\left(\frac{11}{8} \times 72\right) + \left(\frac{125}{5}\right) = 99 + 25 = 124$(this is the answer)

C. $\left(\left(\frac{30}{4} + \frac{13}{2}\right) \times 7\right) - \frac{11}{2} + \frac{110}{4} = \left(\left(\frac{30+26}{4}\right) \times 7\right) - \frac{11}{2} + \frac{55}{2} = \left(\left(\frac{56}{4}\right) \times 7\right) + \frac{55-11}{2} =$

$(14 \times 7) + \frac{44}{2} = 98 + 22 = 120$

D. $(2 \times 10) + (50 \times 1.5) + 15 = 20 + 75 + 15 = 110$

E. $\frac{481}{6} + \frac{121}{3} = \frac{481+242}{6} = 120.5$

4) Answer: E.

six years ago, Amy was two times as old as Mike. Mike is 14 years

now. Therefore, 6 years ago Mike was 8 years.

Six years ago, Amy was: $A = 2 \times 8 = 16$

Now Amy is 22 years old: $16 + 6 = 22$

5) Answer: C.

Set of number that are not composite between 1 and 10: A = {2, 3, 5, 7}

$$\text{Probability} = \frac{number\ of\ desired\ outcomes}{number\ of\ total\ outcomes} = \frac{4}{10} = \frac{2}{5}$$

6) Answer: C.

I. $|a| < 2 \rightarrow -2 < a < 2$

Multiply all sides by b. Since, $b > 0 \rightarrow -2b < ba < 2b$ (it is true!)

II. Since, $-2 < a < 2, and\ a < 0 \rightarrow -a > a^2 > a$ (plug in $-\frac{1}{2}$, and check!) (It's false)

III. $-2 < a < 2, multiply\ all\ sides\ by\ 2, then: -4 < 2a < 4$

Subtract 3 from all sides. Then:

$-4 - 3 < 2a - 3 < 2 - 3 \rightarrow -7 < 2a - 3 < 1$ (It is true!)

7) Answer: A.

Check each option provided:

A. 11 $\qquad \frac{1+4+5+8+12}{5} = \frac{30}{5} = 6$

B. 4 $\qquad \frac{1+5+8+11+12}{5} = \frac{37}{5} = 7.4$

C. 5 $\qquad \frac{1+4+8+11+12}{5} = \frac{36}{5} = 7.2$

D. 1 $\qquad \frac{4+5+11+8+12}{5} = \frac{40}{5} = 8$

E. 12 $\qquad \frac{1+4+5+8+11}{5} = \frac{29}{5} = 5.8$

8) Answer: C.

The weight of 14.2 meters of this rope is: $14.2 \times 600\ g = 8{,}520\ g$

1 kg = 1,000 g, therefore, 8,520 g ÷ 1,000 = 8.52 kg

9) Answer: E.

$y = 4ab + 3b^3$

Plug in the values of a and b in the equation: $a = 3$ and $b = 1$

$y = 4\ (3)\ (1) + 3\ (1)^3 = 12 + 3(1) = 12 + 3 = 15$

10) Answer: D.

$$(g-f)(x) = g(x)-f(x) = (-x^2-5-4x)-(8+x)$$
$$-x^2-5-4x-8-x = -x^2-5x-13$$

11) Answer: B.

To find the discount, multiply the number by (100% – rate of discount).

Therefore, for the first discount we get: (D) (100% – 60%) = (D) (0.40) = 0.40 D

For increase of 10 %: (0.40 D) (100% + 10%) = (0.40 D) (1.10) = 0.44 D = 44% of D

12) Answer: B.

1,000 times the number is 80.5. Let x be the number, then:

$$1,000x = 80.5 \rightarrow x = \frac{80.5}{1,000} = 0.0805$$

13) Answer: A.

Let's review the options provided.

A. 4. In 4 years, David will be 48 and Ava will be 12. 48 is 4 times 12.

B. 6. In 6 years, David will be 50and Ava will be 14. 50 is NOT 4 times 14.

C. 8. In 8 years, David will be 52 and Ava will be 16. 52 is not 4 times 16.

D. 10. In 10 years, David will be 54 and Ava will be 18. 54 is not 4 times 18.

E. 14. In 14 years, David will be 58 and Ava will be 22. 58 is not 4 times 20.

14) Answer: D.

The area of the floor is: 8 cm × 36cm = 288 cm

The number is tiles needed = 288 ÷ 9 = 32

15) Answer: A.

Write the numbers in order:

4, 7, 8, 9, 16, 18, 22

Since we have 7 numbers (7 is odd), then the median is the number in the middle, which is 9.

16) Answer: C.

Employer's revenue: $0.5x + 7,000$

17) Answer: B.

The diagonal of the square is 6. Let x be the side.

Use Pythagorean Theorem: $a^2 + b^2 = c^2$

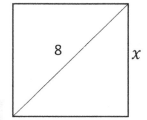

$x^2 + x^2 = 8^2 \Rightarrow 2x^2 = 64 \Rightarrow 2x^2 = 64 \Rightarrow x^2 = 32 \Rightarrow x = \sqrt{32}$

The area of the square is: $\sqrt{32} \times \sqrt{32} = 32$

18) Answer: B.

$x = 40 + 135 = 175$

19) Answer: D.

By definition, the sine of any acute angle is equal to the cosine of its complement.

Since, angle A and B are complementary angles, therefore:

$\sin A = \cos B$

20) Answer: E.

Solve the system of equations by elimination method.

$\begin{aligned} 4x - 3y &= -12 \\ -x + y &= 4 \end{aligned}$ Multiply the second equation by 4, then add it to the first equation.

$\begin{aligned} 4x - 3y &= -12 \\ 4(-x + y &= 4) \end{aligned} \Rightarrow \begin{aligned} 4x - 3y &= -12 \\ -4x + 4y &= 16) \end{aligned} \Rightarrow$ add the equations, $y = 4$

21) Answer: C.

Use distance formula:

Distance = Rate × time $\Rightarrow 248 = 40 \times$ T, divide both sides by 40.

$\frac{248}{40} =$ T $\Rightarrow$ T = 6.2 hours.

Change hours to minutes for the decimal part. 0.2 hours = 0.2 × 60 = 18 minutes.

22) Answer: D.

x and z are colinear. y and $6x$ are colinear. Therefore,

$x + z = y + 6x, subtract\ x\ from\ both\ sides, then, z = y + 5x$

23) Answer: D.

Check each option.

A. $\frac{1}{4} < 0.15$ $\frac{1}{4} = 0.25$ and it is less than 0.15. Not true!

B. $10\% = \frac{3}{5}$ $10\% = \frac{1}{10} < \frac{3}{5}$. Not True!

C. $3 < \frac{3}{2}$ $\frac{3}{2} = 1.5 < 3$. Not True!

D. $\frac{4}{6} > 0.6$ $\frac{4}{6} = 0.6666\dots$ and it is greater than 0.6. Bingo!

E. None of them above   Not True!

24) Answer: C.

40% of 60 equals to: $0.40 \times 60 = 24$

16% of 600 equals to: $0.16 \times 600 = 96$

40% of 60 is added to 16% of 600: $24 + 96 = 120$

25) Answer: D.

The relationship among all sides of special right triangle

$30°, \; 60°, \; 90°$ is provided in this triangle:

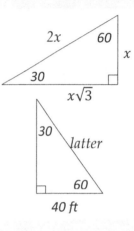

In this triangle, the opposite side of $30°$ angle is half of the

hypotenuse. Draw the shape of this question.

The latter is the hypotenuse.

Therefore, the latter is 80 ft.

26) Answer: A.

The percent of girls playing tennis is: $80 \% \times 15 \% = 0.80 \times 0.15 = 0.12 = 12\%$

27) Answer: D.

Solve for x. $x^3 + 28 = 120 \Rightarrow x^3 = 92$

Let's review the options.

A. 1 and 2. $1^3 = 1$ and $2^3 = 8$, 92 is not between these two numbers.

B. 2 and 3. $2^3 = 8$ and $3^3 = 27$, 92 is not between these two numbers.

C. 3 and 4. $3^3 = 27$ and $4^3 = 64$, 92 is not between these two numbers.

D. 4 and 5. $4^3 = 64$ and $5^3 = 125$, 92 is between these two numbers.

E. 5 and 6. $5^3 = 125$ and $6^3 = 216$, 92 is not between these two numbers.

28) Answer: B.

$(x-3)^3 = 8 \rightarrow x - 3 = 2 \rightarrow x = 5$

$\rightarrow (x-4)(x-3) = (5-4)(5-3) = (1)(2) = 2$

29) Answer: B.

$3x^2 + 4y^5 - x^2 + 3z^3 - 2y^2 + 3x^3 - 3y^5 + 4z^3 = 3x^2 - x^2 + 3x^3 - 2y^2 + 4y^5 -$

$3y^5 + 3z^3 + 4z^3 = 2x^2 + 3x^3 - 2y^2 + y^5 + 7z^3$

30) Answer: A.

Add the first 5 numbers. $40 + 42 + 55 + 38 + 50 = 225$

To find the distance traveled in the next 5 hours, multiply the average by number of hours.

Distance = Average × Rate = $60 \times 5 = 300$

Add both numbers. $300 + 225 = 525$

31) Answer: B.

The question is this: 1.61 is what percent of 1.15?

Use percent formula: part = $\frac{percent}{100} \times$ whole

$1.61 = \frac{percent}{100} \times 1.15 \Rightarrow 1.61 = \frac{percent \times 1.15}{100} \Rightarrow 161 = percent \times 1.15 \Rightarrow percent = \frac{161}{1.15}$

$= 140$

32) Answer: D.

We know that: $i = \sqrt{-1} \Rightarrow i^2 = -1$

$(-3 + 4i)(4 + 5i) = -12 - 15i + 16i + 20i^2 = -12 + i - 20 = i - 32$

33) Answer: B.

$tan\theta = \frac{opposite}{adjacent}$

$tan\theta = \frac{6}{8} \Rightarrow$ we have the following right triangle. Then,

$c = \sqrt{6^2 + 8^2} = \sqrt{36 + 64} = \sqrt{100} = 10$

$cos\theta = \frac{adjacent}{hypotenuse} = \frac{8}{10} = \frac{4}{5}$

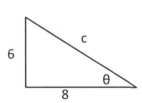

34) Answer: D.

The amplitude in the graph of the equation $y = acosbx$ is a. (a and b are constant)

In the equation $y = cos x$, the amplitude is 2 and the period of the graph is 2π.

The only option that has two times the amplitude of graph $y = cos x$ is $y = 2 + 2cos x$

They both have the amplitude of 2 and period of 2π.

35) Answer: B.

$\frac{1}{3} \cong 0.33$ $\frac{4}{7} \cong 0.57$ $\frac{7}{11} \cong 0.63$ $\frac{3}{4} = 0.75$

36) Answer: A.

Let x be the number of years. Therefore, \$3,000 per year equals $3,000x$.

starting from \$32,000 annual salary means you should add that amount to $3,000x$.

Income more than that is: $I > 3,000\,x + 32,000$.

37) Answer: D.

Percentage of men in city C $= \frac{700}{1,365} \times 100 = 51.28\%$

Percentage of men in city B $= \frac{300}{591} \times 100 = 50.76\%$

Percentage of men in city C to percentage of men in city B: $\frac{51.28}{50.76} = 1.01$

38) Answer: C.

Ratio of women to men in city A: $\frac{570}{600} = 0.95$

Ratio of women to men in city B: $\frac{291}{300} = 0.97$

Ratio of women to men in city C: $\frac{665}{700} = 0.95$

Ratio of women to men in city D: $\frac{528}{550} = 0.96$

39) Answer: B.

Let the number of women should be added to city D be x, then:

$\frac{528 + x}{550} = 1.3 \rightarrow 528 + x = 550 \times 1.3 = 715 \rightarrow x = 187$

40) Answer: B.

We write the numbers in the order: 2, 2, 3, 3, 3, 3, 5, 7, 7, 7, 7

The mode of numbers is: 3 and 7, median is: 3

41) Answer: C.

Let the number be A. Then: $x = y\% \times A \rightarrow$ (Solve for A) $\rightarrow x = \frac{y}{100} \times A$

Multiply both sides by $\frac{100}{y}$: $x \times \frac{100}{y} = \frac{y}{100} \times \frac{100}{y} \times A \rightarrow A = \frac{100x}{y}$

42) Answer: C.

$tangent\ \beta = \frac{1}{cotangent\ \beta} = \frac{1}{1} = 1$

43) Answer: B.

$\frac{4}{5} \times 90 = 72$

44) Answer: B.

One liter $= 1,000 cm^3 \rightarrow$ 6 liters $= 6,000\ cm^3$

$6,000 = 20 \times 5 \times h \rightarrow h = \frac{6,000}{100} = 60$ cm

45) Answer: A.

Surface Area of a cylinder $= 2\pi r\ (r + h)$,

The radius of the cylinder is 2 ($4 \div 2$) inches and its height is 8 inches. Therefore,

Surface Area of a cylinder $= 2\pi\ (2)\ (2 + 8) = 40\ \pi$

46) Answer: C.

3% of the volume of the solution is alcohol. Let x be the volume of the solution.

Then: 3% of $x = 24$ml $\Rightarrow 0.03\ x = 24 \Rightarrow x = 24 \div 0.03 = 800$

47) Answer: B.

$|x - 8| \leq 4 \rightarrow -4 \leq x - 8 \leq 4 \rightarrow -4 + 8 \leq x - 8 + 8 \leq 4 + 8 \rightarrow 4 \leq x \leq 12$

48) Answer: C.

Plug in each pair of number in the equation:

A. $(3, -1)$: $3(3) - (-1) = 10$ Nope!

B. $(-1, 3)$: $3\ (-1) - (3) = 0$ Nope!

C. $(-1, -1)$: $3\ (-1) - (-1) = -2$ Bingo!

D. $(3, -3)$: $3\ (3) - (-3) = 12$ Nope!

E. $(0, -3)$: $3\ (0) - (-3) = 3$ Nope!

49) Answer: A.

The area of ΔBED is 15, then: $\frac{5 \times AB}{2} = 15 \rightarrow 5 \times AB = 30 \rightarrow AB = 6$

The area of ΔBDF is 20, then: $\frac{4 \times BC}{2} = 20 \rightarrow 4 \times BC = 40 \rightarrow BC = 10$

The perimeter of the rectangle is $= 2 \times (6 + 10) = 32$

50) Answer: E.

The slop of line A is: $m = \frac{y_2 - y_1}{x_2 - x_1} = \frac{7-6}{5-4} = 1$

Parallel lines have the same slope and only choice E ($y = x$) has slope of 1.

51) Answer: C.

When points are reflected over y-axis, the value of y in the coordinates doesn't change and the sign of x changes. Therefore, the coordinates of point B is $(-8, 2)$.

52) Answer: D.

If 15 balls are removed from the bag at random, there will be one ball in the bag. The probability of choosing a brown ball is 1 out of 16. Therefore, the probability of not choosing a brown ball is 15 out of 16 and the probability of having not a brown ball after removing 15 balls is the same.

53) Answer: C.

Write a proportion and solve for x.

$\frac{5}{3} = \frac{x}{54} \Rightarrow 3x = 5 \times 54 \Rightarrow x = 90$ ft

54) Answer: B.

The area of trapezoid is: $\left(\frac{12+18}{2}\right) \times x = 120 \rightarrow 15x = 120 \rightarrow x = 8$

$y = \sqrt{8^2 + 6^2} = 10$

Perimeter is: $18 + 8 + 12 + 10 = 48$

55) Answer: E.

$0.8x = (0.2) \times 40 \rightarrow x = 10 \rightarrow (x + 4)^2 = (14)^2 = 196$

56) Answer: D.

$g(x) = -1$, then $f(g(x)) = f(-1) = 3(-1)^3 + 6(-1)^2 + 2(-1) = -3 + 6 - 2 = 1$

57) Answer: B.

Use the information provided in the question to draw the shape.

Use Pythagorean Theorem: $a^2 + b^2 = c^2$

$25^2 + 60^2 = c^2 \Rightarrow 625 + 3{,}600 = c^2$

$\Rightarrow 4{,}225 = c^2 \Rightarrow c = 65$

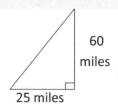

60 miles

25 miles

58) Answer: E.

$$\begin{cases} 2x = x + 3y - 5 \\ 6x = 8y + 10 \end{cases} \rightarrow \begin{cases} x - 3y = -5 \\ 6x - 8y = 10 \end{cases}$$

Multiply first equation by -6.

$$\begin{cases} -6x + 18y = 30 \\ 6x - 8y = 10 \end{cases} \rightarrow \text{add two equations.}$$

$10y = 40 \rightarrow y = 4 \rightarrow x = 7 \rightarrow x \times y = 28$

59) Answer: C.

To solve for $f(2g(p))$, first, find $2g(p)$

$g(x) = log_2 x \rightarrow g(p) = log_2 p \rightarrow 2g(p) = 2log_2 p = log_2 p^2$

Now, find $f(2g(p))$: $f(x) = 2^x \rightarrow f(log_2 p^2) = 2^{log_2 p^2}$

Logarithms and exponentials with the same base cancel each other. This is true because logarithms and exponentials are inverse operations. Then: $f(log_2 p^2) = 2^{log_2 p^2} = p^2$

60) Answer: B.

$$x_1 = \frac{8y + \frac{r}{r+1}}{\frac{10}{\frac{z}{5}}} = \frac{8y + \frac{r}{r+1}}{\frac{5 \times 10}{z}} = \frac{8y + \frac{r}{r+1}}{5 \times \frac{10}{z}} = \frac{1}{5} \times \frac{8y + \frac{r}{r+1}}{\frac{10}{z}} = \frac{x}{5}$$

Answers and Explanations

ACT Mathematics

Practice Tests 4

1) Answer: D.

$640,000 = 6.4 \times 10^5$

2) Answer: A.

$(x^4)^{\frac{5}{8}} = x^{4 \times \frac{5}{8}} = x^{\frac{20}{8}} = x^{\frac{5}{2}}$

3) Answer: A.

To simplify the fraction, multiply both numerator and denominator by i. $\frac{2-5i}{-2i} \times \frac{i}{i} =$

$\frac{2i-5i^2}{-2i^2}$

$i^2 = -1$, Then: $\frac{2i-5i^2}{-2i^2} = \frac{2i-5(-1)}{-2(-1)} = \frac{2i+5}{2} = \frac{2i}{2} + \frac{5}{2} = i + \frac{5}{2}$

4) Answer: B.

$343 = 7^3 \quad \rightarrow 7^x = 7^3 \rightarrow x = 3$

5) Answer: D.

Here is the list of all prime numbers between 10 and 20:

11, 13, 17, 19

The sum of all prime numbers between 10 and 20 is:

$11 + 13 + 17 + 19 = 60$

6) Answer: E.

Solve for x. $\sqrt{5x} = \sqrt{y}$

Square both sides of the equation: $(\sqrt{5x})^2 = (\sqrt{y})^2$

$5x = y \rightarrow x = \frac{y}{5}$

7) Answer: B.

$\text{average} = \frac{\text{sum of terms}}{\text{number of terms}}$

The sum of the weight of all girls is: $30 \times 65 = 1,950$ kg

The sum of the weight of all boys is: $20 \times 60 = 1,200$ kg

The sum of the weight of all students is: $1,950 + 1,200 = 3,150$ kg

average $= \frac{3,150}{50} = 63$

8) Answer: E.

$y = (-3x^3)^2 = (-3)^2(x^3)^2 = 9x^6$

9) Answer: C.

Plug in the value of x and y. $x = 2$ and $y = -3$

$2(x - y) + (1 - x)^2 = 2(2 - (-3)) + (1 - 2)^2 = 2(2 + 3) + (-1)^2 = 11$

10) Answer: B.

The question is this: 406.25 is what percent of 625?

Use percent formula: part $= \frac{\text{percent}}{100} \times$ whole

$406.25 = \frac{\text{percent}}{100} \times 625 \Rightarrow 406.25 = \frac{\text{percent} \times 625}{100} \Rightarrow 40,625 = \text{percent} \times 625 \Rightarrow \text{percent}$

$= \frac{40,625}{625} = 65$

406.25 is 65 % of 625. Therefore, the discount is: $100\% - 65\% = 35\%$

11) Answer: A.

$\left(\frac{f}{g}\right)(x) = \frac{f(x)}{g(x)} = \frac{2x - 5}{x^2 - 4x}$

12) Answer: A.

The equation of a line is: $y = mx + b$, where m is the slope and b is the y-intercept.

First find the slope: $m = \frac{y_2 - y_1}{x_2 - x_1} = \frac{10 - (-5)}{8 - 3} = \frac{15}{5} = 3$

Then, we have: $y = 3x + b$

Choose one point and plug in the values of x and y in the equation to solve for b.

Let's choose the point $(3, -5)$

$y = 3x + b \rightarrow -5 = 3(3) + b \rightarrow -5 = 9 + b \rightarrow b = -14$

The equation of the line is: $y = 3x - 14$

13) Answer: B.

Use simple interest formula:

$I = prt$ (I = interest, p = principal, r = rate, t = time)

$I = (13,000)(0.025)(2) = 650$

14) Answer: E.

Number of visiting fans: $\frac{4 \times 12,000}{6} = 8,000$

15) Answer: E.

The sum of all angles in a quadrilateral is 360 degrees.

Let x be the smallest angle in the quadrilateral. Then the angles are: $x, 3x, 5x, 6x$

$x + 3x + 5x + 6x = 360 \rightarrow 15x = 360 \rightarrow x = 24$

The angles in the quadrilateral are: $24°, 72°, 120°,$ and $144°$

16) Answer: B.

$sin^2 a + cos^2 a = 1$, then:

$x + 1 = 4 \rightarrow x = 3$

17) Answer: C.

Formula for the area of a circle is: $A = \pi r^2$

Using 64 for the area of the circle we have: $64 = \pi r^2$

Let's solve for the radius (r).

$\frac{64}{\pi} = r^2 \rightarrow r = \sqrt{\frac{64}{\pi}} = \frac{8}{\sqrt{\pi}} = \frac{8}{\sqrt{\pi}} \times \frac{\sqrt{\pi}}{\sqrt{\pi}} = \frac{8\sqrt{\pi}}{\pi} \rightarrow d = 2r = 2 \times \frac{8\sqrt{\pi}}{\pi} \rightarrow d = \frac{16\sqrt{\pi}}{\pi}$

18) Answer: C.

Length of the rectangle is: $\frac{3}{4} \times 32 = 24$

perimeter of rectangle is: $2 \times (24 + 32) = 112$

19) Answer: E.

The angle x and 45 are complementary angles. Therefore:

$x + 45 = 180$

$180° - 45° = 135°$

20) Answer: A.

Solving Systems of Equations by Elimination

Multiply the first equation by (–3), then add it to the second equation.

$$\begin{matrix} -3(2x + 3y = 8) \\ 6x - 3y = -24 \end{matrix} \Rightarrow \begin{matrix} -6x - 9y = -24 \\ 6x - 3y = -24 \end{matrix} \Rightarrow -12y = -48 \Rightarrow y = 4$$

Plug in the value of y into one of the equations and solve for x.

$$2x + 3(4) = 8 \Rightarrow 2x + 12 = 8 \Rightarrow 2x = -4 \Rightarrow x = -2$$

21) Answer: A.

The sum of supplement angles is 180. Let x be that angle. Therefore, $x + 5x = 180 \Rightarrow$

$6x = 180$, divide both sides by 6: $x = 30$

22) Answer: D.

Three times of 14,000 is 42,000. One sixth of them cancelled their tickets.

One sixth of 42,000 equal 7,000 ($\frac{1}{6} \times 42,000 = 7,000$).

35,000 (42,000 – 7,000 = 35,000) fans are attending this week

23) Answer: E.

$sin\alpha = \frac{1}{2} \Rightarrow$ Since $sin\alpha = \frac{opposite}{hypotenuse}$, we have the following right triangle. Then,

$c = \sqrt{8^2 - 4^2} = \sqrt{64 - 16} = \sqrt{48}$

$cos\alpha = \frac{\sqrt{48}}{8} = \frac{\sqrt{16} \times \sqrt{3}}{8} = \frac{\sqrt{3}}{2}$

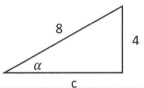

24) Answer: D.

In any rectangle measure of all angles equals 360°.

25) Answer: B.

The equation of a circle in standard form is:

$(x - h)^2 + (y - k)^2 = r^2$, where r is the radius of the circle.

In this circle the radius is 2. $r^2 = 4 \rightarrow r = 2$

$(x + 1)^2 + (y - 2)^2 = 2^2$

Area of a circle: $A = \pi r^2 = \pi (2)^2 = 4\pi$

26) Answer: C.

the population is increased by 25% and 40%. 25% increase changes the population to 125% of original population.

For the second increase, multiply the result by 140%.

$(1.25) \times (1.40) = 1.75 = 175\%$

75 percent of the population is increased after two years.

27) Answer: D.

$6x^2y^3 + 4x^3y^5 - (4x^2y^3 - 3x^3y^5) = 6x^2y^3 - 4x^2y^3 + 4x^3y^5 + 3x^3y^5 = 7x^3y^5 + 2x^2y^3$

28) Answer: E.

Frist factor the function: $f(x) = x^3 + 7x^2 + 12x = x(x+3)(x+4)$

To find the zeros, $f(x)$ should be zero. $f(x) = x(x+3)(x+4) = 0$

Therefore, the zeros are: $x = 0$

$(x+3) = 0 \Rightarrow x = -3$; $(x+4) = 0 \Rightarrow x = -4$

29) Answer: A.

The relationship among all sides of right triangle $30°,\ 60°,\ 90°$ is provided in the following triangle:

Sine of 30° equals to: $\dfrac{opposite}{hypotenuse} = \dfrac{x}{2x} = \dfrac{1}{2}$

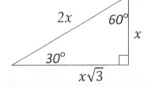

30) Answer: D.

Let x be the length of AB, then: $30 = \dfrac{x \times 5}{2} \rightarrow x = 12$

The length of AC $= \sqrt{12^2 + 16^2} = \sqrt{400} = 20$

The perimeter of $\Delta ABC = 12 + 16 + 20 = 48$

31) Answer: C.

$x_{1,2} = \dfrac{-b \pm \sqrt{b^2 - 4ac}}{2a}$

$ax^2 + bx + c = 0 \Rightarrow 2x^2 + 4x - 10 = 0$, then: a = 2, b = 4 and c = − 10

$x = \dfrac{-4 + \sqrt{4^2 - 4 \times 2 \times (-10)}}{2 \times 2} = \sqrt{6} - 1$; $x = \dfrac{-4 - \sqrt{4^2 - 4 \times 2 \times (-10)}}{2 \times 2} = -1 - \sqrt{6}$

32) Answer: A.

Let x be the cost of one-kilogram orange, then:

$3x + (2 \times 3.6) = 40.2 \rightarrow 3x + 7.2 = 40.2 \rightarrow 3x = 40.2 - 7.2 \rightarrow 3x = 33 \rightarrow x =$
$\frac{33}{3} = \$11$

33) Answer: B.

Simplify the expression.

$$\sqrt{\frac{x^2}{2} + \frac{x^2}{16}} = \sqrt{\frac{8x^2}{16} + \frac{x^2}{16}} = \sqrt{\frac{9x^2}{16}} = \sqrt{\frac{9}{16}x^2} = \sqrt{\frac{9}{16}} \times \sqrt{x^2} = \frac{3}{4} \times x = \frac{3x}{4}$$

34) Answer: D.

First find the number of pants sold in each month.

January: 110, February: 88, March: 90, April: 70, May: 84, June: 65

Check each option provided.

F. There is a decrease from January to February

G. February and March,

$\left(\frac{90-88}{90}\right) \times 100 = \frac{2}{90} \times 100 = 2.22\%$

H. There is a decrease from March to April

I. April and May: there is an increase from April to May

$\left(\frac{84-70}{70}\right) \times 100 = \frac{14}{70} \times 100 = 20\%$

J. There is a decrease from May to June.

35) Answer: C.

First, order the number of shirts sold each month:

$130, 140, 144, 150, 160, 170$

mean is: $\frac{130+140+144+150+160+170}{6} = \frac{894}{6} = 149$

Put the number of shoes sold per month in order:

$20, 25, 25, 35, 35, 40$; median is: $\frac{25+35}{2} = 30$

36) Answer: B.

The ratio of number of pants to number of shoes in May equals $\frac{84}{25}$.

Five-seventeenth of this ratio is $\left(\frac{5}{12}\right)\left(\frac{84}{25}\right)$. Now, let x be the number of shoes needed to be added in April.

$\frac{70}{20+x} = \left(\frac{5}{12}\right)\left(\frac{84}{25}\right) \rightarrow \frac{70}{20+x} = \frac{420}{300} = 1.4 \rightarrow 70 = 1.4(20+x) \rightarrow 70 = 28 + 1.4x \rightarrow$

$1.4x = 42 \rightarrow x = 30$

37) Answer: B.

The probability of choosing a heart is $\frac{13}{52} = \frac{1}{4}$

38) Answer: A.

Let x be the number of shoes the team can purchase. Therefore, the team can purchase $10\,x$.

The team had $20,000 and spent $14,000. Now the team can spend on new shoes $6,000 at most.

Now, write the inequality: $120x + 14,000 \leq 20,000$

39) Answer: A.

Plug in the value of x in the equation and solve for y.

$4y = \frac{2x^2}{3} + 8 \rightarrow 4y = \frac{2(6)^2}{3} + 8 \rightarrow 4y = \frac{2(36)}{3} + 8 \rightarrow 4y = 24 + 8 = 32$

$\rightarrow 4y = 32 \rightarrow y = 8$

40) Answer: E.

Use formula of rectangle prism volume.

$V = $ (length) (width) (height) $\Rightarrow 3,600 = (12)(10)$ (height) $\Rightarrow$ height $= 3,600 \div 120 = 30$

41) Answer: E.

The ratio of boy to girls is 2:6. Therefore, there are 2 boys out of 8 students. To find the answer, first divide the total number of students by 8, then multiply the result by 2.

$400 \div 8 = 50 \Rightarrow 50 \times 2 = 100$

42) Answer: C.

Plug in the value of each option in the inequality.

A. 2 $(2-3)^2 + 1 > 3(2) + 1 \rightarrow 2 > 7$ No!

B. 6 $(6-3)^2 + 1 > 3(6) + 1 \rightarrow 10 > 19$ No!

C. 8 $(8 - 3)^2 + 1 > 3(8) + 1 \rightarrow 26 > 25$ Bingo!

D. 3 $(3 - 3)^2 + 1 > 3(3) + 1 \rightarrow 1 > 10$ No!

E. 4 $(4 - 3)^2 + 1 > 3(4) + 1 \rightarrow 2 > 13$ No!

43) Answer: A.

$(x + 5)(x + p) = x^2 + (5 + p)x + 5p \rightarrow 5 + p = 6 \rightarrow p = 1 \ and \ r = 5p = 5$

44) Answer: C.

First, find the number.

Let x be the number. Write the equation and solve for x.

150% of a number is 75, then:

$1.5 \times x = 75 \Rightarrow x = 75 \div 1.5 = 50$

60% of 50 is: $0.6 \times 50 = 30$

45) Answer: D.

If the length of the box is 45, then the width of the box is one third of it, 15, and the height of the box is 5 (one third of the width). The volume of the box is:

V = (length) × (width) × (height) = (45) × (15) × (5) = 3,375

46) Answer: C.

Let x be the smallest number. Then, these are the numbers:

$x, x + 1, x + 2, x + 3, x + 4$

average $= \dfrac{\text{sum of terms}}{\text{number of terms}} \Rightarrow 34 = \dfrac{x + (x+1) + (x+2) + (x+3) + (x+4)}{5} \Rightarrow 34 = \dfrac{5x + 10}{5} \Rightarrow 170 =$

$5x + 10 \Rightarrow 160 = 5x \Rightarrow x = 32$

47) Answer: D.

Formula for the Surface area of a cylinder is:

$SA = 2\pi r^2 + 2\pi r h \rightarrow 132\pi = 2\pi r^2 + 2\pi r(5) \rightarrow r^2 + 5r - 66 = 0$

Factorize and solve for r.

$(r + 11)(r - 6) = 0 \rightarrow r = 6 \quad or \quad r = -11 \ (unacceptable)$

48) Answer: C.

Since the triangle ABC is reflected over the y-axis, then all values of y's of the points don't change and the sign of all x's change.

(remember that when a point is reflected over the y-axis, the value of y does not change and when a point is reflected over the x-axis, the value of x does not change).

Therefore:

$(4, -2)$ changes to $(-4, -2)$

$(-2, -3)$ changes to $(2, -3)$

$(3, 5)$ changes to $(-3, 5)$

49) Answer: B.

The equation of a line in slope intercept form is: $y = mx + b$

Solve for y.

$9x - 3y = 18 \Rightarrow -3y = 18 - 9x \Rightarrow y = (18 - 9x) \div (-3) \Rightarrow$

$y = 3x - 6 \rightarrow$ The slope is 3.

The slope of the line perpendicular to this line is:

$m_1 \times m_2 = -1 \Rightarrow 3 \times m_2 = -1 \Rightarrow m_2 = -\frac{1}{3}$

50) Answer: B.

The area of rectangle is: $9 \times 5 = 45 \ cm^2$

The area of circle is: $\pi r^2 = \pi \times (\frac{16}{2})^2 = 3 \times 64 = 192 \ cm^2$

Difference of areas is: $192 - 45 = 147$

51) Answer: E.

$f\big(g(x)\big) = 4 \times (\frac{1}{x})^3 + 4 = \frac{4}{x^3} + 4$

52) Answer: D.

Use the information provided in the question to draw the shape. Use Pythagorean Theorem: $a^2 + b^2 = c^2$

$50^2 + 120^2 = c^2 \Rightarrow 2,500 + 14,400 = c^2$

$\Rightarrow 16,900 = c^2 \Rightarrow c = 130$

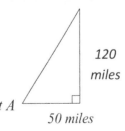

Port A

120 miles

50 miles

53) Answer: C.

Let L be the length of the rectangular and W be the with of the rectangular. Then, $L = 3W + 2$

The perimeter of the rectangle is 36 meters. Therefore:

$$2L + 2W = 36$$

$$L + W = 18$$

Replace the value of L from the first equation into the second equation and solve for W:

$$(3W + 2) + W = 18 \rightarrow 4W + 2 = 18 \rightarrow 4W = 16 \rightarrow W = 4$$

The width of the rectangle is 4 meters and its length is:

$$L = 3W + 2 = 3(4) + 2 = 14$$

The area of the rectangle is: length × width = $14 \times 4 = 56$

54) Answer: B.

Let x be the number of adult tickets and y be the number of student tickets. Then:

$x + y = 16$

$12.50x + 6.50y = 128$

Use elimination method to solve this system of equation. Multiply the first equation by -6.5 and add it to the second equation.

$-6.5(x + y = 16) \Rightarrow -6.5x - 6.5y = -104$

$12.50x + 6.50y = 128 \Rightarrow 6x = 24 \rightarrow x = 4$

There are 4 adults' tickets and 12 student tickets.

55) Answer: A.

$x - 3 \geq 5 \rightarrow x \geq 5 + 3 \rightarrow x \geq 8$

Or $x - 3 \leq -5 \rightarrow x \leq -5 + 3 \rightarrow x \leq -2$

Then, solution is: $x \geq 8 \cup x \leq -2$

56) Answer: B.

$\tan = \frac{opposite}{adjacent}$, and $\tan x = \frac{5}{12}$, therefore, the opposite side of the angle x is 5 and the adjacent side is 12. Let's draw the triangle.

Using Pythagorean theorem, we have:

$$a^2 + b^2 = c^2 \rightarrow 5^2 + 12^2 = c^2 \rightarrow 25 + 144 = c^2 \rightarrow c = 13$$

$$\sin x = \frac{opposite}{hypotenuse} = \frac{5}{13}$$

57) Answer: E.

Based on triangle similarity theorem:

$$\frac{a}{a+b} = \frac{c}{5} \rightarrow c = \frac{5a}{a+b} = \frac{5\sqrt{3}}{\sqrt{3}+4\sqrt{3}} = 1$$

$\rightarrow$ area of shaded region is: $\left(\frac{c+5}{2}\right)(b) = 3 \times 4\sqrt{3} = 12\sqrt{3}$

58) Answer: C.

Write the ratio of $7a$ to $3b$, $\frac{7a}{3b} = \frac{1}{15}$

Use cross multiplication and then simplify.

$$7a \times 15 = 3b \times 1 \rightarrow 105a = 3b \rightarrow a = \frac{3b}{105} = \frac{b}{35}$$

Now, find the ratio of a to b.

$$\frac{a}{b} = \frac{\frac{b}{35}}{b} \rightarrow \frac{b}{35} \div b = \frac{b}{35} \times \frac{1}{b} = \frac{b}{35b} = \frac{1}{35}$$

59) Answer: E.

First, find $2A$.

$$A = \begin{bmatrix} -1 & 3 \\ 1 & -3 \end{bmatrix} \Rightarrow 2A = 2 \times \begin{bmatrix} -1 & 3 \\ 1 & -3 \end{bmatrix} = \begin{bmatrix} -2 & 6 \\ 2 & -6 \end{bmatrix}$$

Now, solve for $2A - B$:

$$\begin{bmatrix} -2 & 6 \\ 2 & -6 \end{bmatrix} - \begin{bmatrix} 5 & 1 \\ -3 & 4 \end{bmatrix} = \begin{bmatrix} -2-5 & 6-1 \\ 2-(-3) & -6-4 \end{bmatrix} = \begin{bmatrix} -7 & 5 \\ 5 & -10 \end{bmatrix}$$

60) Answer: B.

The amplitude in the graph of the equation $y = a\cos bx$ is a. (a and b are constant)

In the equation $y - 1 = 3\cos 2x$, the amplitude is 3.

Answers and Explanations

ACT Mathematics

Practice Tests 5

1) Answer: C.

$$5^{\frac{5}{2}} \times 5^{\frac{1}{2}} = 5^{\frac{5}{2}+\frac{1}{2}} = 5^{\frac{6}{2}} = 5^3$$

2) Answer: D.

Solve for x, $\frac{5x}{36} = \frac{x-2}{6}$

Multiply the second fraction by 6, $\frac{5x}{36} = \frac{6(x-2)}{6\times6}$

Tow denominators are equal. Therefore, the numerators must be equal.

$5x = 6x - 12 \rightarrow -x = -12 \rightarrow x = 12$

3) Answer: B.

Simplify each option provided.

A. $25 - (5 \times 8) + (7 \times 20) = 25 - 40 + 140 = 125$

B. $\left(\frac{10}{7} \times 63\right) + \left(\frac{124}{4}\right) = 90 + 31 = 121$(this is the answer)

C. $\left(\left(\frac{70}{6} + \frac{22}{3}\right) \times 5\right) - \frac{20}{3} + \frac{130}{6} = \left(\left(\frac{70+44}{6}\right) \times 5\right) - \frac{40}{6} + \frac{130}{6} = \left(\left(\frac{114}{6}\right) \times 5\right) +$

$\frac{130-40}{6} = (19 \times 5) + \frac{90}{6} = 95 + 15 = 110$

D. $(3 \times 11) + (42 \times 2.5) - 14 = 33 + 105 - 14 = 124$

E. $\frac{148}{8} + \frac{207}{2} = \frac{148+828}{8} = 122$

4) Answer: E.

five years ago, Amy was three times as old as Mike. Mike is 11 years

now. Therefore, 5 years ago Mike was 6 years.

five years ago, Amy was: $A = 3 \times 6 = 18$

Now Amy is 23 years old: $18 + 5 = 23$

5) Answer: C.

Set of number that are not composite between 1 and 15: A = {2, 3, 5, 7, 11, 13}

Probability $= \frac{number\ of\ desired\ outcomes}{number\ of\ total\ outcomes} = \frac{6}{15} = \frac{2}{5}$

6) Answer: C.

I. $|a| < 3 \rightarrow -3 < a < 3$

Multiply all sides by b. Since, $b > 0 \rightarrow -3b < ba < 3b$ (it is true!)

II. Since, $-3 < a < 3$, and $a < 0 \rightarrow -a > a^2 > a$ (plug in $-\frac{1}{3}$, and check!) (It's false)

III. $-3 < a < 3$, multiply all sides by 3, then: $-9 < 3a < 9$

Subtract 4 from all sides. Then:

$-9 - 4 < 3a - 4 < 9 - 4 \rightarrow -13 < 3a - 4 < 5$ (It is true!)

7) Answer: A.

Check each option provided:

A. 12 $\frac{2+5+6+9+13}{5} = \frac{35}{5} = 7$

B. 5 $\frac{2+6+9+12+13}{5} = \frac{42}{5} = 8.4$

C. 6 $\frac{2+5+9+12+13}{5} = \frac{41}{5} = 8.2$

D. 2 $\frac{5+6+12+9+13}{5} = \frac{45}{5} = 9$

E. 13 $\frac{2+5+6+9+12}{5} = \frac{34}{5} = 6.8$

8) Answer: C.

The weight of 15.5 meters of this rope is: 15.5×800 g = 124,000 g

1 kg = 1,000 g, therefore, 124,000 g ÷ 1,000 = 124 kg

9) Answer: E.

$y = 2ab + 5b^2$

Plug in the values of a and b in the equation: $a = 4$ and $b = 2$

$y = 2\,(4)\,(2) + 5\,(2)^2 = 16 + 5(4) = 16 + 20 = 36$

10) Answer: D.

$$(g-f)(x) = g(x) - f(x) = (-2x^2 - 6 - x) - (2 + 3x)$$

$$-2x^2 - 6 - x - 2 - 3x = -2x^2 - 4x - 8$$

11) Answer: B.

To find the discount, multiply the number by (100% – rate of discount).

Therefore, for the first discount we get: (D) (100% – 70%) = (D) (0.30) = 0.30 D

For increase of 15 %: (0.30 D) (100% + 15%) = (0.30 D) (1.15) = 0.345 D = 34.5% of

D

12) Answer: B.

100 times the number is 64.7. Let x be the number, then:

$$100x = 64.7 \rightarrow x = \frac{64.7}{100} = 0.647$$

13) Answer: A.

Let's review the options provided.

A. 5. In 5 years, David will be 75 and Ava will be 15. 75 is 5 times 15.

B. 7. In 7 years, David will be 77 and Ava will be 17. 77 is NOT 5 times 17.

C. 9. In 9 years, David will be 79 and Ava will be 19. 79 is not 5 times 19.

D. 12. In 12 years, David will be 82 and Ava will be 22. 82 is not 5 times 22.

E. 15. In 15 years, David will be 85 and Ava will be 25. 85 is not 5 times 25.

14) Answer: D.

The area of the floor is: 7 cm × 33cm = 231 cm

The number is tiles needed = 231 ÷ 11 = 21

15) Answer: A.

Write the numbers in order:

5, 9, 11, 15, 19, 24, 32

Since we have 7 numbers (7 is odd), then the median is the number in the middle,

which is 15.

16) Answer: C.

Employer's revenue: $0.6x + 8,000$

17) Answer: B.

The diagonal of the square is 6. Let x be the side.

Use Pythagorean Theorem: $a^2 + b^2 = c^2$

$x^2 + x^2 = 6^2 \Rightarrow 2x^2 = 36 \Rightarrow 2x^2 = 36 \Rightarrow x^2 = 18 \Rightarrow x = \sqrt{18}$

The area of the square is: $\sqrt{18} \times \sqrt{18} = 18$

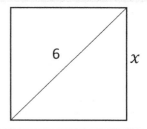

18) Answer: B.

$x = 50 + 125 = 175$

19) Answer: D.

By definition, the sine of any acute angle is equal to the cosine of its complement.

Since, angle A and B are complementary angles, therefore:

$\cos A = \sin B$

20) Answer: E.

Solve the system of equations by elimination method.

$\begin{array}{l} 2x - 5y = -8 \\ -x + 2y = 3 \end{array}$ Multiply the second equation by 2, then add it to the first equation.

$\begin{array}{l} 2x - 5y = -8 \\ 2(-x + 2y = 3) \end{array} \Rightarrow \begin{array}{l} 2x - 5y = -8 \\ -2x + 4y = 6 \end{array} \Rightarrow$ add the equations, $y = 2$

21) Answer: C.

Use distance formula:

Distance = Rate × time $\Rightarrow 312 = 60 \times T$, divide both sides by 40.

$\frac{312}{60} = T \Rightarrow T = 5.2$ hours.

Change hours to minutes for the decimal part. 0.2 hours = $0.2 \times 60 = 18$ minutes.

22) Answer: D.

x and z are colinear. y and $6x$ are colinear. Therefore,

$x + z = y + 7x, subtract\ x\ from\ both\ sides, then, z = y + 6x$

23) Answer: D.

Check each option.

A. $\frac{1}{5} < 0.16$ $\frac{1}{4} = 0.20$ and it is less than 0.16. Not true!

B. $20\% = \frac{2}{10}$ $20\% = \frac{1}{5} < \frac{4}{5}$. Not True!

C. $4 < \frac{7}{3}$ $\frac{7}{3} = 2.333 < 4$. Not True!

D. $\frac{5}{8} > 0.625$ $\frac{5}{8} = 0.625$ and it is greater than 0.59. Bingo!

E. None of them above   Not True!

24) Answer: C.

30% of 70 equals to: $0.30 \times 70 = 21$

18% of 500 equals to: $0.18 \times 500 = 90$

30% of 70 is added to 18% of 500: $21 + 90 = 111$

25) Answer: D.

The relationship among all sides of special right triangle

$30°$, $60°$, $90°$ is provided in this triangle:

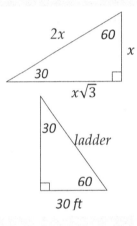

In this triangle, the opposite side of $30°$ angle is half of the

hypotenuse. Draw the shape of this question.

The ladder is the hypotenuse.

Therefore, the ladder is 60 ft.

26) Answer: A.

The percent of girls playing tennis is: $75\% \times 12\% = 0.75 \times 0.12 = 0.09 = 9\%$

27) Answer: D.

Solve for x. $x^3 + 52 = 170 \Rightarrow x^3 = 118$

Let's review the options.

A. 1 and 2. $1^3 = 1$ and $2^3 = 8$, 118 is not between these two numbers.

B. 2 and 3. $2^3 = 8$ and $3^3 = 27$, 118 is not between these two numbers.

C. 3 and 4. $3^3 = 27$ and $4^3 = 64$, 118 is not between these two numbers.

D. 4 and 5. $4^3 = 64$ and $5^3 = 125$, 118 is between these two numbers.

E. 5 and 6. $5^3 = 125$ and $6^3 = 216$, 118 is not between these two numbers.

28) Answer: B.

$(x - 5)^2 = 9 \rightarrow x - 5 = 3 \rightarrow x = 8$

$\rightarrow (x - 6)(x - 5) = (8 - 6)(8 - 5) = (2)(3) = 6$

29) Answer: B.

$4x^2 + 5y^5 - 2x^2 + 5z^3 - y^2 + 4x^3 - 2y^5 + 3z^3 = 4x^2 - 2x^2 + 4x^3 - y^2 + 5y^5 - 2y^5 + 5z^3 + 3z^3 = 2x^2 + 4x^3 - y^2 + 3y^5 + 8z^3$

30) Answer: A.

Add the first 4 numbers. $44 + 46 + 42 + 52 = 184$

To find the distance traveled in the next 4 hours, multiply the average by number of hours.

Distance = Average × Rate = $55 \times 4 = 220$

Add both numbers. $220 + 184 = 404$

31) Answer: B.

The question is this: 3.06 is what percent of 2.04?

Use percent formula: part $= \frac{\text{percent}}{100} \times$ whole

$3.06 = \frac{\text{percent}}{100} \times 2.04 \Rightarrow 3.06 = \frac{\text{percent} \times 2.04}{100} \Rightarrow 306 = \text{percent} \times 2.04 \Rightarrow \text{percent} = \frac{306}{2.04}$

$= 150$

32) Answer: D.

We know that: $i = \sqrt{-1} \Rightarrow i^2 = -1$

$(-2 + 3i)(5 + 6i) = -10 - 12i + 15i + 18i^2 = -10 + 3i - 18 = 3i - 28$

33) Answer: B.

$tan\theta = \frac{\text{opposite}}{\text{adjacent}}$

$tan\theta = \frac{5}{12} \Rightarrow$ we have the following right triangle. Then,

$c = \sqrt{5^2 + 12^2} = \sqrt{25 + 144} = \sqrt{169} = 13$

$cos\theta = \frac{adjacent}{hypotenuse} = \frac{12}{13}$

34) Answer: D.

The amplitude in the graph of the equation $y = asinbx$ is a. (a and b are constant)

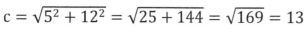

In the equation $y = sinx$, the amplitude is 1 and the period of the graph is 2π.

The only option that has five times the amplitude of graph $y = sin\ x$ is $y = 5 + 5sin\ 2x$ for the half period $sin2x = sin2\pi \Rightarrow 2x = 2\pi \Rightarrow x = \pi$

They both have the amplitude of 5 and period of π.

35) Answer: B.

$\frac{2}{5} = 0.4$, $\frac{1}{2} = 0.5$, $\frac{8}{13} \cong 0.61$, $\frac{5}{7} \cong 0.71$

36) Answer: A.

Let x be the number of years. Therefore, \$4,000 per year equals $4,000x$.

starting from \$36,000 annual salary means you should add that amount to $4,000x$.

Income more than that is: $I > 4,000\ x + 36,000$.

37) Answer: D.

Percentage of men in city C $= \frac{710}{1,385} \times 100 = 51.26\%$

Percentage of men in city B $= \frac{320}{631} \times 100 = 50.71\%$

Percentage of men in city C to percentage of men in city B: $\frac{51.26}{50.71} = 99.11$

38) Answer: C.

Ratio of women to men in city A: $\frac{520}{550} = 0.95$

Ratio of women to men in city B: $\frac{311}{320} = 0.97$

Ratio of women to men in city C: $\frac{675}{710} = 0.95$

Ratio of women to men in city D: $\frac{548}{570} = 0.96$

39) Answer: B.

Let the number of women should be added to city D be x, then:

$\frac{548 + x}{570} = 1.4 \rightarrow 548 + x = 570 \times 1.4 = 798 \rightarrow x = 228$

40) Answer: B.

We write the numbers in the order: 4, 4, 5, 5, 5, 5, 6, 8, 8, 8, 8

The mode of numbers is: 5 and 8, median is: 5

41) Answer: C.

Let the number be A. Then: $y = x\% \times A \rightarrow$ (Solve for A) $\rightarrow x = \frac{x}{100} \times A$

Multiply both sides by $\frac{100}{x}$: $y \times \frac{100}{x} = \frac{x}{100} \times \frac{100}{x} \times A \rightarrow A = \frac{100y}{x}$

42) Answer: D.

$tangent\ \beta = \frac{1}{cotangent\ \beta} = \frac{1}{\sqrt{2}} = \frac{\sqrt{2}}{2}$

43) Answer: B.

$\frac{3}{8} \times 96 = 36$

44) Answer: B.

One liter=$1,000 cm^3 \rightarrow 8$ liters = $8,000\ cm^3$

$8,000 = 40 \times 2 \times h \rightarrow h = \frac{8,000}{80} = 100$ cm

45) Answer: A.

Surface Area of a cylinder = $2\pi r\ (r\ +\ h)$,

The radius of the cylinder is 3 ($6 \div 2$) inches and its height is 10 inches. Therefore,

Surface Area of a cylinder = $2\pi\ (3)\ (3 + 10) = 78\ \pi$

46) Answer: C.

4% of the volume of the solution is alcohol. Let x be the volume of the solution.

Then: 4% of $x = 28$ml $\Rightarrow 0.04\ x = 28 \Rightarrow x = 28 \div 0.04 = 700$

47) Answer: B.

$|x - 5| \leq 2 \rightarrow -2 \leq x - 5 \leq 2 \rightarrow -2 + 5 \leq x - 5 + 5 \leq 2 + 5 \rightarrow 3 \leq x \leq 7$

48) Answer: C.

Plug in each pair of number in the equation:

   A. $(1, -2)$: $2(1) - 3(-2) = 8$ Nope!

   B. $(-3, 0)$: $2\ (-3) - 3(0) = -6$ Nope!

   C. $(-2, -3)$: $2\ (-2) - 3\ (-3) = 5$ Bingo!

   D. $(1, -4)$: $2\ (1) - 3\ (-4) = 14$ Nope!

   E. $(0, -2)$: $2\ (0) - 3\ (-2) = 6$ Nope!

49) Answer: A.

The area of ΔBED is 18, then: $\frac{6 \times AB}{2} = 18 \rightarrow 6 \times AB = 36 \rightarrow AB = 6$

The area of ΔBDF is 10, then: $\frac{2 \times BC}{2} = 10 \rightarrow 2 \times BC = 20 \rightarrow BC = 10$

The perimeter of the rectangle is $= 2 \times (6 + 10) = 32$

50) Answer: E.

The slop of line A is: $m = \frac{y_2 - y_1}{x_2 - x_1} = \frac{9 - 8}{3 - 2} = 1$

Parallel lines have the same slope and only choice E ($y = x$) has slope of 1.

51) Answer: C.

When points are reflected over y-axis, the value of y in the coordinates doesn't change and the sign of x changes. Therefore, the coordinates of point B is $(-7, 3)$.

52) Answer: D.

If 18 balls are removed from the bag at random, there will be one ball in the bag. The probability of choosing a brown ball is 1 out of 17. Therefore, the probability of not choosing a brown ball is 17 out of 18 and the probability of having not a brown ball after removing 17 balls is the same.

53) Answer: C.

Write a proportion and solve for x.

$\frac{7}{6} = \frac{x}{48} \Rightarrow 6x = 7 \times 48 \Rightarrow x = 56$ ft

54) Answer: B.

The area of trapezoid is: $\left(\frac{13 + 22}{2}\right) \times x = 210 \rightarrow 17.5x = 210 \rightarrow x = 12$

$y = \sqrt{9^2 + 12^2} = 15$

Perimeter is: $22 + 12 + 13 + 15 = 62$

55) Answer: E.

$0.6x = (0.3) \times 30 \rightarrow x = 15 \rightarrow (x + 3)^2 = (18)^2 = 324$

56) Answer: D.

$g(x) = -2,$

then $f(g(x)) = f(-2) = 2(-2)^3 + 3(-2)^2 + (-2) = -16 + 12 - 2 = -6$

57) Answer: B.

Use the information provided in the question to draw the shape.

Use Pythagorean Theorem: $a^2 + b^2 = c^2$

$15^2 + 36^2 = c^2 \Rightarrow 225 + 1{,}296 = c^2$

$\Rightarrow 1{,}521 = c^2 \Rightarrow c = 39$

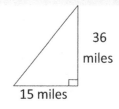

36 miles

15 miles

58) Answer: E.

$\begin{cases} 3x = 2x + y - 5 \\ 4x = 3y - 12 \end{cases} \rightarrow \begin{cases} x - y = -5 \\ 4x - 3y = -12 \end{cases}$

Multiply first equation by -4.

$\begin{cases} -4x + 4y = 20 \\ 4x - 3y = -12 \end{cases} \rightarrow$ add two equations.

$y = 8 \rightarrow y = 8 \rightarrow x = 3 \rightarrow x \times y = 24$

59) Answer: C.

To solve for $f(5g(p))$, first, find $5g(p)$

$g(x) = \log_5 x \rightarrow g(p) = \log_5 p \rightarrow 5g(p) = 5\log_5 p = \log_5 p^5$

Now, find $f(5g(p))$: $f(x) = 5^x \rightarrow f(\log_5 p^5) = 5^{\log_5 p^5}$

Logarithms and exponentials with the same base cancel each other. This is true because logarithms and exponentials are inverse operations. Then: $f(\log_5 p^5) = 5^{\log_5 p^5} = p^5$

60) Answer: B.

$$x_1 = \frac{7y + \frac{r}{2r+3}}{\frac{z}{6}} = \frac{7y + \frac{r}{2r+3}}{\frac{6 \times 12}{z}} = \frac{7y + \frac{r}{2r+3}}{6 \times \frac{12}{z}} = \frac{1}{6} \times \frac{7y + \frac{r}{2r+3}}{\frac{12}{z}} = \frac{x}{6}$$

Answers and Explanations
ACT Mathematics
Practice Tests 6

1) Answer: D.

$7,800,000 = 7.8 \times 10^6$

2) Answer: A.

$(x^3)^{\frac{4}{9}} = x^{3 \times \frac{4}{9}} = x^{\frac{12}{9}} = x^{\frac{4}{3}}$

3) Answer: A.

To simplify the fraction, multiply both numerator and denominator by i. $\frac{3-4i}{-3i} \times \frac{i}{i} =$

$\frac{3i-4i^2}{-3i^2}$

$i^2 = -1$, Then: $\frac{3i-4i^2}{-3i^2} = \frac{3i-4(-1)}{-3(-1)} = \frac{3i+4}{3} = \frac{3i}{3} + \frac{4}{3} = i + \frac{4}{3}$

4) Answer: B.

$512 = 8^3 \quad \to 8^x = 8^3 \to x = 3$

5) Answer: D.

Here is the list of all prime numbers between 1 and 10:

$2, 3, 5, 7$

The sum of all prime numbers between 1 and 10 is:

$2 + 3 + 5 + 7 = 17$

6) Answer: E.

Solve for x. $\sqrt{7x} = \sqrt{y}$

Square both sides of the equation: $(\sqrt{7x})^2 = (\sqrt{y})^2$

$7x = y \to x = \frac{y}{7}$

7) Answer: B.

$\text{average} = \frac{\text{sum of terms}}{\text{number of terms}}$

The sum of the weight of all girls is: $24 \times 50 = 1,200 \text{ kg}$

The sum of the weight of all boys is: $26 \times 55 = 1{,}430$ kg

The sum of the weight of all students is: $1{,}200 + 1{,}430 = 2{,}630$ kg

$$\text{average} = \frac{2{,}630}{50} = 52.6$$

8) Answer: E.

$$y = (-2x^4)^3 = (-2)^3(x^4)^3 = -8x^{12}$$

9) Answer: C.

Plug in the value of x and y. $x = 3$ and $y = -1$

$$4(x + y) + (2 - x)^2 = 4(3 + (-1)) + (2 - 3)^2 = 4(3 - 1) + (-1)^2 = 9$$

10) Answer: B.

The question is this: 235.80 is what percent of 524?

Use percent formula: $\text{part} = \frac{\text{percent}}{100} \times \text{whole}$

$235.80 = \frac{\text{percent}}{100} \times 524 \Rightarrow 235.80 = \frac{\text{percent} \times 524}{100} \Rightarrow 23{,}580 = \text{percent} \times 524 \Rightarrow \text{percent}$

$= \frac{23{,}580}{524} = 45$

235.80 is 45 % of 524. Therefore, the discount is: $100\% - 45\% = 65\%$

11) Answer: A.

$$\left(\frac{f}{g}\right)(x) = \frac{f(x)}{g(x)} = \frac{3x - 8}{2x^2 - 5x}$$

12) Answer: A.

The equation of a line is: $y = mx + b$, where m is the slope and b is the y-intercept.

First find the slope: $m = \frac{y_2 - y_1}{x_2 - x_1} = \frac{8 - (-7)}{6 - 1} = \frac{15}{5} = 3$

Then, we have: $y = 3x + b$

Choose one point and plug in the values of x and y in the equation to solve for b.

Let's choose the point $(1, -7)$

$$y = 3x + b \rightarrow -7 = 3(1) + b \rightarrow -7 = 3 + b \rightarrow b = -10$$

The equation of the line is: $y = 3x - 10$

13) Answer: B.

Use simple interest formula:

$I = prt$ (I = interest, p = principal, r = rate, t = time)

$I = (15,000)(0.015)(3) = 675$

14) Answer: E.

Number of visiting fans: $\frac{5 \times 16,000}{8} = 10,000$

15) Answer: E.

The sum of all angles in a quadrilateral is 360 degrees.

Let x be the smallest angle in the quadrilateral. Then the angles are: $x, 3x, 7x, 9x$

$x + 3x + 7x + 9x = 360 \rightarrow 20x = 360 \rightarrow x = 18$

The angles in the quadrilateral are: $18°, 54°, 126°$, and $162°$

16) Answer: B.

$2sin^2a + 2cos^2a = 2(sin^2a + cos^2a) = 2(1) = 2$, then:

$x + 2 = 6 \rightarrow x = 4$

17) Answer: C.

Formula for the area of a circle is: $A = \pi r^2$

Using 100 for the area of the circle we have: $100 = \pi r^2$

Let's solve for the radius (r).

$\frac{100}{\pi} = r^2 \rightarrow r = \sqrt{\frac{100}{\pi}} = \frac{10}{\sqrt{\pi}} = \frac{10}{\sqrt{\pi}} \times \frac{\sqrt{\pi}}{\sqrt{\pi}} = \frac{10\sqrt{\pi}}{\pi} \rightarrow d = 2r = 2 \times \frac{10\sqrt{\pi}}{\pi} \rightarrow d = \frac{20\sqrt{\pi}}{\pi}$

18) Answer: C.

Length of the rectangle is: $\frac{4}{5} \times 40 = 32$

perimeter of rectangle is: $2 \times (32 + 40) = 144$

19) Answer: E.

The angle x and 45 are complementary angles. Therefore:

$x + 55 = 180$

$180° - 55° = 125°$

20) Answer: A.

Solving Systems of Equations by Elimination

Multiply the first equation by (–4), then add it to the second equation.

$$\begin{array}{c} -4(x + 2y = 7) \\ 4x + 5y = 22 \end{array} \Rightarrow \begin{array}{c} -4x - 8y = -28 \\ 4x + 5y = 22 \end{array} \Rightarrow -3y = -6 \Rightarrow y = 2$$

Plug in the value of y into one of the equations and solve for x.

$$x + 2(2) = 7 \Rightarrow x + 4 = 7 \Rightarrow x = 7 - 4 \Rightarrow x = 3$$

21) Answer: A.

The sum of supplement angles is 180. Let x be that angle. Therefore, $x + 4x = 180 \Rightarrow$

$5x = 180$, divide both sides by 5: $x = 36$

22) Answer: D.

Two times of 15,000 is 30,000. One fifth of them cancelled their tickets.

One fifth of 30,000 equal 6,000 ($\frac{1}{5} \times 30,000 = 6,000$).

24,000 (30,000 – 6,000 = 24,000) fans are attending this week

23) Answer: E.

$sin\alpha = \frac{\sqrt{3}}{2} \Rightarrow$ Since $sin\alpha = \frac{opposite}{hypotenuse}$, we have the following right triangle. Then,

$$c = \sqrt{2^2 - (\sqrt{3})^2} = \sqrt{4 - 3} = \sqrt{1} = 1$$

$$cos\alpha = \frac{1}{2}$$

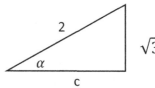

24) Answer: D.

In any squares measure of all angles equals 360°.

25) Answer: B.

The equation of a circle in standard form is:

$(x - h)^2 + (y - k)^2 = r^2$, where r is the radius of the circle.

In this circle the radius is 3. $r^2 = 9 \rightarrow r = 3$

$(x + 2)^2 + (y - 1)^2 = 3^2$

Area of a circle: $A = \pi r^2 = \pi(3)^2 = 9\pi$

26) Answer: C.

the population is increased by 15% and 30%. 15% increase changes the population to 115% of original population.

For the second increase, multiply the result by 130%.

$(1.15) \times (1.30) = 1.495 = 149.5\%$

49.5 percent of the population is increased after two years.

27) Answer: D.

$8x^5y^2 + 3x^3y^4 - (2x^5y^2 - 4x^3y^4) = 8x^5y^2 - 2x^5y^2 + 3x^3y^4 + 4x^3y^4 =$

$6x^5y^2 + 7x^3y^4$

28) Answer: E.

Frist factor the function: $f(x) = 2x^3 + 14x^2 + 20x = 2x(x+2)(x+5)$

To find the zeros, $f(x)$ should be zero. $f(x) = 2x(x+2)(x+5) = 0$

Therefore, the zeros are: $x = 0$

$(x+2) = 0 \Rightarrow x = -2 \;;\; (x+5) = 0 \Rightarrow x = -5$

29) Answer: A.

The relationship among all sides of right triangle $30°$, $60°$, $90°$ is provided in the following triangle:

Sine of $60°$ equals to: $\dfrac{opposite}{hypotenuse} = \dfrac{x\sqrt{3}}{2x} = \dfrac{\sqrt{3}}{2}$

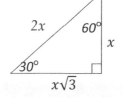

30) Answer: D.

Let x be the length of AB, then: $45 = \dfrac{x \times 6}{2} \to x = 15$

The length of AC $= \sqrt{15^2 + 20^2} = \sqrt{625} = 25$

The perimeter of $\Delta ABC = 15 + 20 + 25 = 60$

31) Answer: C.

$x_{1,2} = \dfrac{-b \pm \sqrt{b^2 - 4ac}}{2a}$

$ax^2 + bx + c = 0 \Rightarrow 3x^2 + 5x - 8 = 0$, then: a = 3, b = 5 and c = -8

$x = \dfrac{-5 + \sqrt{5^2 - 4 \times 3 \times (-8)}}{2 \times 3} = 1 \;;\; x = \dfrac{-5 - \sqrt{5^2 - 4 \times 3 \times (-8)}}{2 \times 3} = -\dfrac{8}{3}$

32) Answer: A.

Let x be the cost of one-kilogram orange, then:

$4x + (3 \times 2.4) = 51.2 \rightarrow 4x + 7.2 = 51.2 \rightarrow 4x = 51.2 - 7.2 \rightarrow 4x = 44 \rightarrow x = \frac{44}{4} = \$11$

33) Answer: B.

Simplify the expression.

$\sqrt{\frac{3x^2}{5} + \frac{x^2}{25}} = \sqrt{\frac{15x^2}{25} + \frac{x^2}{25}} = \sqrt{\frac{16x^2}{25}} = \sqrt{\frac{16}{25}x^2} = \sqrt{\frac{16}{25}} \times \sqrt{x^2} = \frac{4}{5} \times x = \frac{4x}{5}$

34) Answer: D.

First find the number of pants sold in each month.

January: 100, February: 78, March: 80, April: 60, May: 74, June: 55

Check each option provided.

K. There is a decrease from January to February

L. February and March,

$\left(\frac{80-78}{80}\right) \times 100 = \frac{2}{80} \times 100 = 2.5\%$

M. There is a decrease from March to April

N. April and May: there is an increase from April to May

$\left(\frac{74-60}{74}\right) \times 100 = \frac{14}{74} \times 100 = 18.92\%$

O. There is a decrease from May to June.

35) Answer: C.

First, order the number of shirts sold each month:

$120, 130, 135, 140, 150, 160$

mean is: $\frac{120+130+135+140+150+160}{6} = \frac{834}{6} = 139$

Put the number of shoes sold per month in order:

$15, 20, 20, 30, 30, 35$; median is: $\frac{20+30}{2} = 25$

36) Answer: B.

The ratio of number of pants to number of shoes in March equals $\frac{80}{35}$.

Seven-eighth of this ratio is $\left(\frac{7}{8}\right)\left(\frac{80}{35}\right)$. Now, let x be the number of shoes needed to be added in February.

$\frac{78}{30+x} = \left(\frac{7}{8}\right)\left(\frac{80}{35}\right) \rightarrow \frac{78}{30+x} = \frac{560}{280} = 2 \rightarrow 78 = 2(30+x) \rightarrow 78 = 60 + 2x \rightarrow 2x = 18 \rightarrow x = 9$

37) **Answer: B.**

The probability of choosing a heart or diamonds is $\frac{26}{52} = \frac{1}{2}$

38) **Answer: A.**

Let x be the number of shoes the team can purchase. Therefore, the team can purchase $110\,x$.

The team had $25,000 and spent $18,000. Now the team can spend on new shoes $7,000 at most.

Now, write the inequality: $110x + 18,000 \leq 25,000$

39) **Answer: A.**

Plug in the value of x in the equation and solve for y.

$5y = \frac{3x^2}{8} + 9 \rightarrow 5y = \frac{3(4)^2}{8} + 9 \rightarrow 5y = \frac{3(16)}{8} + 9 \rightarrow 5y = 6 + 9 = 15$

$\rightarrow 5y = 15 \rightarrow y = 3$

40) **Answer: E.**

Use formula of rectangle prism volume.

V = (length) (width) (height) $\Rightarrow 4,800 = (8)(15)$ (height) $\Rightarrow$ height = $4,800 \div 120 = 40$

41) **Answer: E.**

The ratio of boy to girls is 3:7. Therefore, there are 3 boys out of 10 students. To find the answer, first divide the total number of students by 10, then multiply the result by 3.

$320 \div 10 = 32 \Rightarrow 32 \times 3 = 96$

42) **Answer: C.**

Plug in the value of each option in the inequality.

A. 1 $(1-2)^2 + 3 > 2(1) + 3 \rightarrow 4 > 5$ No!

B. 5 $(5-2)^2 + 3 > 2(5) + 3 \rightarrow 12 > 13$ No!

C. 7 $(7-2)^2 + 3 > 2(7) + 3 \rightarrow 28 > 17$ Bingo!

D. 2 $(2-2)^2 + 3 > 2(2) + 3 \rightarrow 3 > 7$ No!

E. 3 $(3-2)^2 + 3 > 2(3) + 3 \rightarrow 4 > 9$ No!

43) Answer: A.

$(x+3)(x+p) = x^2 + (3+p)x + 3p \rightarrow 3 + p = 4 \rightarrow p = 1 \ and \ r = 3p = 3$

44) Answer: C.

First, find the number.

Let x be the number. Write the equation and solve for x.

140% of a number is 70, then:

$1.4 \times x = 70 \Rightarrow x = 70 \div 1.4 = 50$

80% of 50 is: $0.8 \times 50 = 40$

45) Answer: D.

If the length of the box is 20, then the width of the box is half of it, 10, and the height of the box is 5 (half of the width). The volume of the box is:

V = (length) × (width) × (height) = (20) × (10) × (5) = 1,000

46) Answer: C.

Let x be the smallest number. Then, these are the numbers:

$x, x+1, x+2, x+3, x+4, x+5$

average $= \frac{\text{sum of terms}}{\text{number of terms}} \Rightarrow 24 = \frac{x+(x+1)+(x+2)+(x+3)+(x+4)+(x+5)}{5} \Rightarrow 24 = \frac{6x+15}{6} \Rightarrow 144$

$= 6x + 15 \Rightarrow 129 = 6x \Rightarrow x = 21.5$

47) Answer: D.

Formula for the Surface area of a cylinder is:

$SA = 2\pi r^2 + 2\pi rh \rightarrow 120\pi = 2\pi r^2 + 2\pi r(7) \rightarrow r^2 + 7r - 60 = 0$

Factorize and solve for r.

$(r+12)(r-5) = 0 \rightarrow r = 5 \quad or \quad r = -12 \ (unacceptable)$

48) Answer: C.

Since the triangle ABC is reflected over the y-axis, then all values of y's of the points don't change and the sign of all x's change.

(remember that when a point is reflected over the y-axis, the value of y does not change and when a point is reflected over the x-axis, the value of x does not change).

Therefore:

$(5, -1)$ changes to $(-5, -1)$

$(-4, -2)$ changes to $(4, -2)$

$(2, 4)$ changes to $(-2, 4)$

49) Answer: B.

The equation of a line in slope intercept form is: $y = mx + b$

Solve for y.

$8x - 2y = 16 \Rightarrow -2y = 16 - 8x \Rightarrow y = (16 - 8x) \div (-2) \Rightarrow$

$y = 4x - 8 \rightarrow$ The slope is 4.

The slope of the line perpendicular to this line is:

$m_1 \times m_2 = -1 \Rightarrow 4 \times m_2 = -1 \Rightarrow m_2 = -\frac{1}{4}$

50) Answer: B.

The area of rectangle is: $8 \times 4 = 32 \ cm^2$

The area of circle is: $\pi r^2 = \pi \times (\frac{12}{2})^2 = 3 \times 36 = 108 \ cm^2$

Difference of areas is: $108 - 32 = 76$

51) Answer: E.

$f(g(x)) = 4 \times (\frac{2}{x})^3 + 5 = \frac{32}{x^3} + 5$

52) Answer: D.

Use the information provided in the question to draw the shape. Use Pythagorean Theorem: $a^2 + b^2 = c^2$

$21^2 + 28^2 = c^2 \Rightarrow 441 + 784 = c^2$

$\Rightarrow 1,225 = c^2 \Rightarrow c = 35$

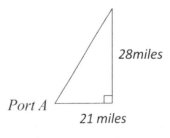

53) Answer: C.

Let L be the length of the rectangular and W be the with of the rectangular. Then, $L = 7W + 5$

The perimeter of the rectangle is 90 meters. Therefore:

$$2L + 2W = 90$$

$$L + W = 45$$

Replace the value of L from the first equation into the second equation and solve for W:

$$(7W + 5) + W = 45 \rightarrow 8W + 5 = 45 \rightarrow 8W = 40 \rightarrow W = 5$$

The width of the rectangle is 4 meters and its length is:

$$L = 7W + 5 = 7(5) + 5 = 40$$

The area of the rectangle is: length × width = 40 × 5 = 200

54) Answer: B.

Let x be the number of adult tickets and y be the number of student tickets. Then:

$$x + y = 18$$

$$10.50x + 5.50y = 119$$

Use elimination method to solve this system of equation. Multiply the first equation by -5.5 and add it to the second equation.

$$-5.5(x + y = 18) \Rightarrow -5.5x - 5.5y = -99$$

$$10.50x + 5.50y = 119 \Rightarrow 5x = 20 \rightarrow x = 4$$

There are 4 adults' tickets and 14 student tickets.

55) Answer: A.

$$x - 4 \geq 7 \rightarrow x \geq 7 + 4 \rightarrow x \geq 11$$

Or $x - 4 \leq -7 \rightarrow x \leq -7 + 4 \rightarrow x \leq -3$

Then, solution is: $x \geq 11 \ \cup \ x \leq -3$

56) Answer: B.

$\tan = \frac{opposite}{adjacent}$, and $\tan x = \frac{15}{20}$, therefore, the opposite side of the angle x is 15 and the adjacent side is 20. Let's draw the triangle.

Using Pythagorean theorem, we have:

$$a^2 + b^2 = c^2 \rightarrow 15^2 + 20^2 = c^2 \rightarrow 225 + 400 = c^2 \rightarrow c = 25$$

$$\sin x = \frac{opposite}{hypotenuse} = \frac{15}{25} = \frac{3}{5}$$

57) Answer: E.

Based on triangle similarity theorem:

$$\frac{a}{a+b} = \frac{c}{3} \rightarrow c = \frac{3a}{a+b} = \frac{3\sqrt{2}}{\sqrt{2}+2\sqrt{2}} = 1$$

$\rightarrow$ area of shaded region is: $\left(\frac{c+3}{2}\right)(b) = \frac{4}{2} \times 2\sqrt{2} = 4\sqrt{2}$

58) Answer: C.

Write the ratio of $9a$ to $8b$, $\frac{9a}{8b} = \frac{1}{16}$

Use cross multiplication and then simplify.

$9a \times 16 = 8b \times 1 \rightarrow 144a = 8b \rightarrow a = \frac{8b}{144} = \frac{b}{18}$

Now, find the ratio of a to b.

$\frac{a}{b} = \frac{\frac{b}{18}}{b} \rightarrow \frac{b}{18} \div b = \frac{b}{18} \times \frac{1}{b} = \frac{b}{18b} = \frac{1}{18}$

59) Answer: E.

First, find $3A$.

$A = \begin{bmatrix} 1 & 1 \\ 2 & -1 \end{bmatrix} \Rightarrow 3A = 3 \times \begin{bmatrix} 1 & 1 \\ 2 & -1 \end{bmatrix} = \begin{bmatrix} 3 & 3 \\ 6 & -3 \end{bmatrix}$

Now, solve for $3A - B$:

$\begin{bmatrix} -3 & 3 \\ 6 & -3 \end{bmatrix} - \begin{bmatrix} 4 & 2 \\ -2 & 3 \end{bmatrix} = \begin{bmatrix} -3-4 & 3-2 \\ 6-(-2) & -3-3 \end{bmatrix} = \begin{bmatrix} -7 & 1 \\ 8 & -6 \end{bmatrix}$

60) Answer: B.

The amplitude in the graph of the equation $y = acosbx$ is a. (a and b are constant)

In the equation $y - 2 = 5cos2x$, the amplitude is 5.

"End"

Made in the USA
Monee, IL
29 November 2021

83351937R00103